200
Salads

Melissa Barlow and
Stephanie Ashcraft

For all my little ones—Izzie, Tate, and Emmy.   —M.B.

To my mother and hero, who trusted me in the
kitchen at a young age and survived raising eight
children who turned out fairly amazing due to all
her hard work and dedication.   —S.A.

First Edition
16 15 14 13 12   5 4 3 2 1

Text © 2012 Melissa Barlow and Stephanie Ashcraft

Published by
Gibbs Smith
P.O. Box 667
Layton, Utah 84041

1.800.835.4993 orders
www.gibbs-smith.com

Designed by Renee Bond
Printed and bound in China

Gibbs Smith books are printed on either recycled, 100% post-
consumer waste, FSC-certified papers or on paper produced
from sustainable PEFC-certified forest/controlled wood source.
Learn more at www.pefc.org.

Library of Congress Cataloging-in-Publication Data

Barlow, Melissa.
  200 salads / Melissa Barlow and Stephanie Ashcraft. — 1st ed.
     p. cm.
  ISBN 978-1-4236-2468-4
1. Salads. 2. Cookbooks. I. Ashcraft, Stephanie. II. Title. III. Title:
Two hundred salads.
  TX740.B37623 2012
  641.83—dc23
                                    2011039880

Contents

Helpful Hints

1. Green-leaf salads should be assembled close to serving time. Dressings should be added right before serving to prevent salads from wilting.

2. To reduce calories, use low-fat or nonfat products.

3. Dip sliced, diced, or chopped pears, apples, and bananas in lemon juice to prevent them from turning brown.

4. Don't store tomatoes in the refrigerator. They last longer and taste fresher when stored on the kitchen counter out of direct sunlight. Do not wash tomatoes until ready to serve.

5. Bigger bowls work best for evenly tossing salads. To toss a salad, add ingredients, place a lid on the bowl, and give the bowl a few gentle shakes.

6. To remove dirt and sand, soak leafy greens in ice-cold water right after they are brought home from the store. Lay greens over paper towels to dry. Place dry greens in an airtight bag lined with a paper towel and store in the vegetable compartment of the refrigerator until ready to serve. Use these cleaned greens within five days to assure freshness,

7. Salad spinners work well to clean lettuce. Simply tear your lettuce into bite-size pieces and drop into the spinner. Run cool water over the top of the torn lettuce, place the lid on the spinner, and spin at will. Your lettuce will come out clean and dry.

8. Thoroughly wash fruits and vegetables before peeling and cutting them. Berries and fruits grown on trees should not be washed until you are ready to use them.

9. Cut cherry tomatoes and grapes in half before adding them to salads. Remember, bite-size pieces are easier for everyone to eat.

10. To keep cooked pastas from sticking together while cooling, sprinkle with a little olive oil and toss to coat. Or, once pasta has cooled, splash with some cold water and it will easily separate.

11. Fresh heads of lettuce last longer than bagged, ready-to-serve lettuce.

12. Most green-leaf salads are more aesthetically pleasing as individual servings instead of a large serving bowl.

13. When cooking meats to use in salads, don't be afraid to season them well—even if the recipe doesn't call for it. Adding a few different spices can give your meat and salad a more robust flavor.

14. Food Cooperatives, Community Supported Agriculture (CSAs), and Farmers Markets are great ways to get fresh produce in season at a bargain price.

Fruit Salads

Citrus-Glazed Fruit Salad

Makes 6–8 servings

Glaze

6 tablespoons frozen orange juice concentrate, thawed

$1/2$ cup water

$1/8$ teaspoon vanilla extract

Salad

1 large green apple

1 large banana

2 oranges

3 kiwifruits

1 cup sliced strawberries

1 cup seedless red grapes

In a small bowl, combine glaze ingredients and set aside.

Cut apple and banana into bite-size pieces and add to glaze. Toss to coat to prevent browning.

Peel and cut oranges into slices and place in a large bowl. Peel and slice kiwifruits then cut slices in half; add to bowl. Add remaining fruit and glaze and stir to coat. Chill 1–2 hours before serving.

Pomegranate Salad

Makes 10–12 servings

1 large box cherry or black cherry gelatin
2 cups boiling water
2 cups cold pomegranate juice
1 (8-ounce) container frozen whipped topping, thawed
1/2 cup sliced almonds or chopped walnuts
1/2–1 cup fresh pomegranate seeds*

In a large bowl, dissolve gelatin in boiling water. Add pomegranate juice. Pour into a 9 x 13-inch dish and chill until set. Spread whipped topping over top and then sprinkle with nuts and pomegranate seeds.

*If pomegranate is not in season, just eliminate.

Pineapple Fruit Salad

Makes **8–10** *servings*

**1 (20-ounce) can
    pineapple chunks,
    with juice**

**1 (8-ounce) can crushed
    pineapple, with juice**

**3/4 cup fat-free plain
    yogurt**

**1 small box instant
    French vanilla or
    cheesecake pudding***

**2 cups fresh or frozen
    blueberries**

2–3 bananas, sliced

**2 cups sliced fresh
    strawberries**

**2 peaches, peeled and
    thinly sliced**

**2 cups seedless green
    or red grapes**

Reserve juice from pineapple chunks. Place pineapple in refrigerator until ready to use. Combine reserved juice, crushed pineapple with juice, yogurt, and dry pudding mix in a medium bowl. Chill for 1–2 hours to allow flavors to blend.

In a large glass bowl, layer the pineapple chunks, blueberries (if frozen, thaw and drain first), bananas, strawberries, peaches, and grapes. Spoon pudding mixture over top.

NOTE: Cut grapes in half if serving to young children.

*Sugar-free pudding can be substituted.

Layered Fruit Salad

Makes 4–6 *servings*

- 1 (6-ounce) container strawberry yogurt
- 4 ounces cream cheese, softened
- 2 tablespoons sugar
- 1 teaspoon lemon juice
- 2 cups cantaloupe chunks
- 2 cups sliced strawberries
- 2 cups sliced kiwifruits
- 1 pint fresh raspberries

In a small bowl, mix yogurt, cream cheese, sugar, and lemon juice with a hand mixer until smooth. Chill until ready to use.

In a glass trifle bowl, spread cantaloupe over bottom. Arrange strawberries over top, followed by kiwifruits, and finishing with raspberries. Evenly spread yogurt mixture over top and serve.

Puckered-Up Citrus Salad

Makes 4–6 *servings*

- 2 oranges
- 2 small grapefruit
- 2 cups pineapple chunks
- 1 pomegranate, seeded*
- 1 lime, thinly sliced

Peel and cut oranges and grapefruit into bite-size pieces and place in a large bowl. Stir in pineapple chunks and pomegranate seeds. Garnish with lime slices.

*2 cups red grapes may be substituted or added in addition to pomegranate seeds.

Orange-Berry Salad

Makes 10–12 servings

1 large box raspberry or
   strawberry gelatin
2 cups boiling water
1 (12-ounce) package
   frozen raspberries
2 bananas, sliced
¾ cup chopped pecans
   or walnuts
1 orange, juiced

In a large bowl, dissolve gelatin in boiling water. Add frozen berries and stir until thawed. Add bananas, nuts, and orange juice. Mix well and chill until set.

Melon Delight Salad

Makes 10–12 servings

1 seedless watermelon*
2 cantaloupe
1 honeydew melon
3–4 cups seedless red
   grapes

Cut melons in half, remove seeds from cantaloupe and honeydew, and, using a melon baller, scoop out balls from each melon. Place balls into a large bowl. Stir in grapes and serve.

*Once flesh is scooped out of watermelon the rind shell may be used as the serving bowl.

Peaches and Cream

Makes 10–12 *servings*

1 large box peach
    gelatin
2 cups boiling water
2 cups cold water
3–4 fresh peaches,
    pitted, peeled, and
    diced*
1 (8-ounce) container
    frozen whipped
    topping, thawed

Dissolve gelatin in boiling water in a medium bowl. Add cold water and then pour into a 9 x 13-inch pan. Chill until partially set, about 45 minutes to 1 hour, and then stir in fruit. Chill until set. Spread whipped topping over top.

*2–3 (15-ounce) cans of peaches, drained and diced, may be substituted.

Mango Fruit Salad

Makes 4–6 *servings*

1 pound strawberries
1 pound grapes, halved
3 kiwifruits, peeled and
    sliced
1 mango, peeled, seeded,
    and sliced

Wash strawberries and grapes. Remove stems and cut each strawberry in half or quarters depending on size. Combine all fruit in a large bowl. Serve immediately. Store any leftovers in the refrigerator.

Mango, Craisin, and Apple Salad

Makes 2–3 servings

1 large mango
1 medium apple
3 tablespoons craisins
1 tablespoon apple cider
    vinegar
1/4 teaspoon ground
    cinnamon
1 pinch salt
1/2 cup cashew pieces

Peel and cube the mango then place in a small bowl with a lid. Core and dice the apple. Add apple, craisins, vinegar, cinnamon, and salt to bowl. Cover and toss until evenly distributed. Chill until ready to serve. Sprinkle cashews over top just before serving.

Sparkling Berry Salad

Makes 9 servings

1 large box blackberry
    fusion gelatin*
1½ cups boiling water
1½ cups lemon-lime soda
3 cups fresh mixed
    berries or frozen
    mixed berries, thawed
1 (8-ounce) container
    frozen whipped
    topping, thawed

In an 8 x 8-inch pan, dissolve gelatin in boiling water. Stir in soda. Chill until partially set, about 45 minutes to 1 hour. Add fruit and then chill until set. Spread whipped topping over top.

*Any berry flavor gelatin may be substituted.

Poppy Seed–Cantaloupe Salad

Makes 6–8 servings

1 medium cantaloupe, cut into bite-size pieces
1–1½ cups seedless grapes, halved
½ cup poppy seed dressing
¼ cup sliced green onions
½ cup real bacon bits

In a large bowl, toss cantaloupe and grapes together. Refrigerate until ready to serve. Before serving, toss salad with poppy seed dressing. Sprinkle green onions and bacon over top.

Honey-Lime Fruit Salad

Makes 6 *servings*

4 cups pineapple chunks
1 (15-ounce) can
   mandarin oranges,
   drained
2 large bananas, sliced
1 pound sliced
   strawberries
6 kiwifruits, peeled
   and sliced

Dressing

1/4 cup lime juice
1 tablespoon honey
1/4 cup pineapple juice
1–2 tablespoons lime
   zest

In a large bowl, toss all fruit together.

In a small bowl, combine lime juice, honey, pineapple juice, and lime zest. Pour over fruit and stir to coat. Chill before serving.

Strawberry-Kiwi Salad

Makes 9 servings

1 large box strawberry-
kiwi gelatin
2 cups boiling water
1½ cups ice
1 banana, thinly sliced
12–14 strawberries,
sliced
1 (8-ounce) container
frozen whipped
topping, thawed
4 kiwifruit, peeled and
thinly sliced

In a medium bowl, dissolve gelatin in boiling water. Stir in ice and then refrigerate until partially set, about 45 minutes.

Stir in banana. Pour into an 8 x 8-inch pan and then chill until firm.

Place a layer of strawberries over set gelatin. Spread whipped topping over strawberries and then garnish with kiwifruit slices over top.

Melon with Strawberries

Makes 10–12 servings

1 large box watermelon
gelatin
2 cups boiling water
2 cups cold water
1 (8-ounce) container
frozen whipped
topping, thawed
2 cups sliced fresh
strawberries

In a large bowl, dissolve gelatin in boiling water. Add cold water. Pour into a 9 x 13-inch pan and chill until firm. Spread whipped topping over gelatin and then top with strawberries.

Piña Colada Fruit Salad

Makes 6–8 servings

1 pound strawberries
1 fresh pineapple
2 cups seedless green
grapes, halved
1 (15-ounce) can
mandarin oranges,
drained
2–3 (6-ounce) containers
piña colada yogurt
$^1/_2$ cup shredded
coconut, optional

Wash, hull, and cut strawberries into bite-size pieces.

Cut off the top and bottom of the pineapple, remove the skin, slice, and cut out the core. Cut the pineapple into chunks.

In a large bowl, combine strawberries, pineapple chunks, grapes, and mandarin oranges. Carefully stir in yogurt and coconut, if desired.

Dr. Pepper Salad

Makes 12 servings

1 (16-ounce) can sweet
  black cherries
1 tablespoon fresh
  lemon juice
2 small boxes black
  cherry gelatin
1 (12-ounce) can cold
  Dr. Pepper
1 (8-ounce) can crushed
  pineapple
1/2 pint whipping
  cream, whipped and
  sweetened

Drain liquid from cherries and reserve. Slice cherries in half and set aside.

Combine reserved liquid with lemon juice and enough water to make 2 cups. Place in a medium saucepan and bring to a boil. Completely dissolve gelatin in boiling liquid and then stir in Dr. Pepper. Pour into a 9 x 13-inch pan and refrigerate until gelatin turns syrupy, about 45 minutes.

Fold cherries and pineapple with juice into the gelatin. Chill until firm. Top with whipped cream.

Coca-Cola Salad

1 (16-ounce) can Bing cherries
1 large box cherry gelatin
1 (12-ounce) can cold Coca-Cola
1 (20-ounce) can crushed pineapple
1 cup chopped walnuts

Drain liquid from cherries and reserve. Slice cherries in half and set aside. Add enough water to cherry juice to make 2 cups. Place in a medium saucepan and bring to a boil. In a 9 x 13-inch pan, pour boiling liquid over gelatin. Stir to dissolve, at least 2 minutes. Stir in Coca-Cola. Refrigerate until partially set, about 45 minutes. Fold in cherries, pineapple with juice, and walnuts. Chill until set.

Cran-Apple Salad

Makes 9 servings

1 small box strawberry gelatin
1 (16-ounce) can whole-berry cranberry sauce
1½ cups chunky applesauce

In a medium bowl, dissolve gelatin in boiling water according to package directions. Stir in cranberry sauce until smoothly blended. Stir in applesauce. Pour into an 8 x 8-inch pan and chill until firm.

Cran-Raspberry Layers

Makes 9 servings

1 large box raspberry gelatin
1¾ cups boiling water
1 (20-ounce) can crushed pineapple
1 (16-ounce) can whole-berry cranberry sauce
1 cup sour cream

In a large bowl, dissolve gelatin in boiling water. Add pineapple with juice and cranberry sauce, stirring until cranberry sauce is well blended. Chill until partially set, about 45 minutes. Pour half of the gelatin mixture into an 8 x 8-inch pan. Chill until firm. Let the remaining gelatin stand at room temperature. Stir in the sour cream and then spread evenly over the firm gelatin. Chill until firm. Cut into squares and serve.

Simple Raspberry Squares

Makes 12 servings

1 large box raspberry gelatin
2 cups boiling water
1 (12-ounce) package frozen raspberries
2 cups cold water
½ pint whipping cream, whipped and sweetened
½ cup chopped walnuts

In a large bowl, dissolve gelatin in boiling water, stirring at least 2 minutes. Add frozen berries and stir until thawed. Add cold water and pour into a 9 x 13-inch pan. Chill until set. Top with whipped cream and sprinkle with chopped walnuts. Cut into squares and serve.

Raspberry Parfait Salad

Makes 12–15 *servings*

1 large box raspberry gelatin
1/2 pint whipping cream, whipped and sweetened
1 pint fresh raspberries

Make gelatin according to package directions and then pour into a glass trifle bowl to set. When gelatin is set, top with whipped cream and decorate with fresh berries.

Raspberry Orange Salad

Makes 9 *servings*

1 small box raspberry gelatin
1 (11-ounce) can mandarin oranges, drained
2 cups fresh raspberries

Make gelatin according to package directions. Chill in a medium bowl, about 30–45 minutes. When partially set, gently fold in oranges and raspberries. Chill until firm.

Tropical Jewel Salad

Makes 9 servings

1 (11-ounce) can
  mandarin oranges
1 (8-ounce) can
  pineapple tidbits
1 small box orange
  gelatin
1 cup cold water
¼ cup flaked coconut,
  optional

Drain mandarin oranges and pineapple; reserve juice. In a small saucepan, combine juices and water to make 1 cup, if needed, and bring to a boil. Pour boiling mixture into gelatin in a medium bowl and stir until completely dissolved, at least 2 minutes. Add cold water. Pour into an 8 x 8-inch pan and chill until partially set, about 30–40 minutes. Gently fold in fruit and coconut, if using. Return to refrigerator until completely set.

Apricot Parfait Salad

Makes 12 servings

2 (15-ounce) cans diced
  apricots
2 small boxes apricot
  gelatin
½ teaspoon lemon
  extract
2 cups cold water
½ pint whipping
  cream, whipped and
  sweetened
½ cup chopped walnuts

Drain apricots and reserve juice. In a small saucepan, add enough water to reserved juice to make 2 cups and bring to a boil. Dissolve gelatin in hot liquid, stirring constantly for at least 2 minutes. Stir in lemon extract and then cold water. Pour into a large glass bowl or trifle bowl, and chill until set. When gelatin is completely set, gently top with drained apricots. Top with whipped cream and then garnish with walnuts.

Creamy Fruit Salads

Orange Creamsicle Fruit Salad

Makes 8–10 *servings*

1 (20-ounce) can
  pineapple chunks,
  with juice
1 (15-ounce) can sliced
  peaches, with juice
1 small box instant
  vanilla pudding*
3 tablespoons Tang
  breakfast drink mix
4 cups fresh or frozen
  blueberries
1 cup seedless green or
  red grapes, halved
1½ cups sliced fresh
  strawberries
2–3 medium bananas,
  sliced

Thoroughly drain pineapple and peaches, reserving all juice. Combine juices, dry pudding mix, and Tang in a medium bowl. Refrigerate until pudding thickens.

In a large bowl, combine pineapple, peaches, blueberries (if frozen, thaw and drain first), grapes, strawberries, and bananas. Fold pudding mixture into fruit. Serve immediately.

*Sugar-free pudding can be substituted.

Melissa's Creamy Fruit Salad

Makes 6–8 servings

1 large peach
4 kiwifruits
1 large banana
2 large Fuji or Gala
 apples
1½ cups sliced
 strawberries
1 cup halved seedless
 red or green grapes
1 (6-ounce) container
 blackberry yogurt
1–1½ cups whipped
 topping

Peel and cut the peach, then place in a large bowl. Peel and slice kiwifruits and banana and add to bowl. Cut apples into bite-size pieces and add to bowl. Gently stir in strawberries and grapes.

In a small bowl, fold yogurt and whipped topping together, then gently stir into fruit. Add more whipped topping, if needed.

Blueberry Cream Cheese Salad

Makes 12 *servings*

2 small boxes raspberry gelatin

2 cups boiling water

1 (16-ounce) can blueberries

1 (8-ounce) can crushed pineapple

1 (8-ounce) package cream cheese, softened

1 pint whipping cream, whipped and sweetened

In a large bowl, dissolve gelatin in boiling water. Stir in blueberries and pineapple with their juice. Mash in cream cheese with a fork or potato masher until mostly blended. Chill in a 9 x 13-inch pan until partially set, about 40 minutes. Fold half the whipped cream into the salad and chill until completely set. Top with remaining whipped cream before serving.

Cool Pear Salad

Makes 8–10 servings

- 1 (29-ounce) can pears, juice reserved
- 1 small box lime or lemon gelatin
- 1 cup hot pear juice (use reserved juice)
- 1 (8-ounce) package cream cheese, room temperature
- 4 tablespoons milk
- 2 cups frozen whipped topping, thawed

In a medium bowl, mash pears with fork. In a small bowl, dissolve gelatin in hot pear juice and let sit until soupy. (Make up the difference with water if there isn't enough pear juice in the can.)

In a large bowl, mash cream cheese and milk with a fork or spoon until smooth. Combine pears, gelatin mixture, and cream cheese mixture. Fold in 1 cup whipped topping. Spoon into a serving bowl and smooth top. Chill at least 2 hours, or until firm. Spread remaining whipped topping over top and serve.

Fresh Fruit and Custard Salad

Makes 6–8 servings

1 cup sliced strawberries

1–2 bananas, sliced and
   halved

1 cup seedless red grapes
   (halved if large)

1 sweet red apple,
   chopped

1½ cups fresh pineapple
   pieces

2 (6-ounce) containers
   Yoplait strawberry
   or vanilla custard
   yogurt, stirred
   smooth

Combine all ingredients in a large
bowl and chill for 1–2 hours before
serving.

Berries and Crème Salad

Crème

1 cup heavy whipping cream
1/2 cup sugar
1 teaspoon unflavored gelatin
1 tablespoon cold water
1/8 cup boiling water
1 cup light sour cream
1 teaspoon vanilla

Salad

2 cups frozen blackberries
2 cups frozen raspberries
1–2 cups halved strawberries,
1 cup blueberries

In a small saucepan, heat cream and sugar together until sugar is dissolved. In a small bowl, combine gelatin with cold water, then boiling water. Combine cream mixture and gelatin mixture in a bowl. With a spoon, whip in sour cream and vanilla. Refrigerate 24 hours or overnight.

Gently layer berries into a 9 x 13-inch pan. Cover and refrigerate 24 hours or overnight. When frozen berries thaw, the juices blend together and make a tart sauce. When ready to serve, remove berries and crème from refrigerator. Gently mix fruit to ensure it is completely covered in sauce. Drizzle crème over top as desired, or serve individual portions by first spooning berries into parfait glasses, then drizzling with crème.

Berry Yogurt Parfait Salad

Makes 4–6 servings

3 cups plain fat-free yogurt

1 small box instant sugar-free cheesecake or white chocolate pudding*

1 (16-ounce) bag frozen berry medley, divided

1/2 tablespoon sugar-free sweetener

1 teaspoon fresh lemon juice

1/2 cup Grape-Nuts or granola, optional

In a large bowl, beat yogurt and dry pudding mix 1–2 minutes with an electric mixer until well blended. Stir in 2 cups of the berries. Place in a 2-quart serving bowl or 8 x 8-inch dish. Refrigerate until ready to serve.

Thaw and mash remaining berries. Stir in sweetener and lemon juice. Spoon berry mixture over salad. Garnish individual servings with Grape-Nuts or granola, if desired.

*Regular pudding mix can be substituted.

Strawberry and Sour Cream Salad

Makes 8 *servings*

1 large box strawberry gelatin

1 cup boiling water

1 box frozen strawberries, partially thawed

1 (8-ounce) can crushed pineapple, drained

2 bananas, mashed

Walnuts

1–1½ cups sour cream

Mix gelatin and boiling water in a large bowl then add strawberries. Next add pineapple, bananas, and walnuts. Pour half the mixture into a large serving bowl and spread sour cream over top. Pour remaining gelatin mixture over top. Chill until set.

Creamy Strawberry Salad

Makes 12 *servings*

1 large box strawberry gelatin

3½ cups boiling water

2 (16-ounce) packages frozen strawberries, thawed

1 pint whipping cream, whipped and sweetened

In a large bowl, dissolve gelatin in boiling water. Stir in strawberries. Chill in a 9 x 13-inch pan until partially set, about 40 minutes. Fold in half the whipped cream. Chill until completely set. Top with remaining whipped cream and serve.

Strawberry-Banana Salad

Makes 4–6 *servings*

**1 pound fresh
    strawberries**
**1/2 pound seedless green
    or red grapes**
**2–3 bananas, peeled and
    sliced**
**1 (8-ounce) container
    strawberry yogurt***
Whipped topping

Wash strawberries and grapes. Remove stems and cut each strawberry in half. Cut grapes in half. Place strawberries and grapes in a medium serving bowl. Add sliced bananas. Stir in yogurt. Serve immediately. Garnish individual servings with a dollop of whipped topping.

*Lemon, vanilla, or strawberry-banana flavored yogurt can also be used.

Dad's Favorite Fruit Salad

Makes 6–8 *servings*

**1 small box strawberry
    gelatin**
1 large banana, sliced
**1½ cups sliced
    strawberries**
1 cup blueberries
**2–3 cups miniature
    marshmallows**
**1 (8-ounce) container
    frozen whipped
    topping, thawed**

Make gelatin in a large bowl according to package directions. Once set, layer banana, strawberries, blueberries, and marshmallows over top and then stir together. Gently fold in whipped topping until well coated.

Double-Layer Citrus Salad

Makes 12–14 *servings*

1 large box orange
   gelatin
1 small box cook-and-
   serve lemon pudding
3 (15-ounce) cans
   mandarin oranges,
   drained
1 small box lemon
   instant pudding
1 (8-ounce) container
   frozen whipped
   topping, thawed

Make orange gelatin according to package directions and then set aside, but do not put in refrigerator to set. Make the cook-and-serve lemon pudding according to package directions.

In a large bowl, combine liquid orange gelatin and cooked lemon pudding with a wire whisk or hand mixer until smooth.

Layer the mandarin oranges in the bottom of a 9 x 13-inch glass dish (extra deep if available). Next pour the gelatin-pudding mixture over top and smooth with a spoon. Refrigerate overnight until set.

Make the lemon instant pudding according to package directions. Fold the whipped topping into the pudding and then spread over the set gelatin-pudding mixture. Refrigerate 1–2 more hours before serving.

Grandma's Raspberry Cream Salad

Makes 8–10 servings

- 1 small box raspberry gelatin
- 1 small box cook-and-serve vanilla pudding
- 3 tablespoons quick-cooking tapioca
- 3 cups cold water
- 1 cup frozen raspberries
- 1 (12-ounce) container frozen whipped topping, thawed and divided

In a medium saucepan, combine dry gelatin, pudding mix, and tapioca; add water. Bring to a boil, stirring constantly. Boil 2 minutes and then remove from heat and stir in frozen raspberries. Cool to room temperature. Transfer salad to a 2-quart glass bowl. Gently fold in whipped topping, reserving some to garnish top. Refrigerate until ready to serve.

Lemonade Salad

1 large box lemon
   gelatin
2 cups boiling water
1 cup sugar
$1/2$ teaspoon salt
1 (12-ounce) can frozen
   lemonade concen-
   trate, slightly thawed
1 (12-ounce) container
   frozen whipped
   topping, thawed
4–6 kiwifruit, peeled
   and thinly sliced

In a large bowl, dissolve gelatin in boiling water. Add sugar and salt. Add lemonade and stir until melted. Refrigerate until syrupy, about 45 minutes to 1 hour. Fold in a little more than half of the whipped topping and pour into a 9 x 13-inch pan. Refrigerate until set and then spread remaining whipped topping over top. Arrange sliced kiwifruit over whipped topping.

Low-Fat Autumn Apple Salad

Makes 5–6 *servings*

1 cup cold fat-free milk
1 small box instant sugar-free butterscotch pudding
1 (8-ounce) container frozen fat-free whipped topping, thawed and divided
3½ cups unpeeled apple chunks
½ cup chopped peanuts or pecans, optional

In a medium bowl, whisk together the milk and dry pudding mix for at least 1 minute until thick. Fold in half of the whipped topping and then fold in apple chunks. Spread remaining whipped topping over salad. Garnish with nuts, if desired. Cover and refrigerate until ready to serve.

NOTE: Regular pudding, milk, or whipped topping can be used as well.

Cherry Waldorf Salad

Makes 4–6 *servings*

1 large Granny Smith apple
1 large Fuji apple
1/2 cup dried cherries, chopped
1/2 cup chopped pecans, divided
2 (6-ounce) containers cherry yogurt

Cut apples into bite-size pieces and mix in a medium bowl with dried cherries and half the pecans. Stir in yogurt and sprinkle remaining nuts over top.

Grape-Nuts Salad

Makes 10–12 *servings*

1 (8-ounce) package cream cheese, softened
1 cup sour cream
1/2 cup sugar
1 teaspoon vanilla
2 pounds green seedless grapes
2 pounds red seedless grapes
1 cup Grape-Nuts cereal
Brown sugar

In a large bowl, combine cream cheese, sour cream, sugar, and vanilla with a hand mixer. Stir in grapes until completely coated. Sprinkle Grape-Nuts over top to cover, then sprinkle brown sugar evenly over Grape-Nuts.

Raspberry Lemonade Salad

Makes 10–12 servings

1 (12-ounce) package
  frozen raspberries,
  thawed
1 large box raspberry
  gelatin
2 cups boiling water
1 pint vanilla ice cream
1 (6-ounce) can frozen
  pink lemonade
  concentrate, thawed
1 (8-ounce) container
  frozen whipped
  topping, thawed

Drain raspberries, reserving syrup. In a large bowl, dissolve gelatin in boiling water. Stir in ice cream by the spoonful until melted. Stir in lemonade concentrate and reserved syrup. Refrigerate in a 9 x 13-inch pan until partially set, about 45 minutes. Fold in raspberries. Refrigerate until firmly set and then spread whipped topping over top. Cut into squares before serving.

Pineapple-Lime Salad

Makes 8–10 *servings*

1 small box lime gelatin
1 (16-ounce) container
    cottage cheese
1 (8-ounce) can crushed
    pineapple
1 (8-ounce) container
    frozen whipped
    topping, thawed
1/2 cup chopped walnuts

In a large bowl, stir dry gelatin mix into cottage cheese. Stir in pineapple with juice. Fold in whipped topping and nuts. Transfer to a serving bowl and chill for at least 4 hours before serving.

Almond Cran-Apple Salad

Makes 3–4 *servings*

3 green apples, cored
    and diced*
1/3 cup dried cranberries
1/4 cup dried cherries,
    chopped
1 (8-ounce) container
    vanilla yogurt
1/4 cup sliced almonds

In a medium serving bowl, mix together apples, cranberries, cherries, and yogurt. Sprinkle almond slices over the salad. Serve immediately or store in refrigerator.

*To prevent apples from changing color, dip in lemon juice.

Creamy Pear and Pineapple Salad

Makes 7–9 servings

1 (29-ounce) can pears, juice reserved

1 (8-ounce) can crushed pineapple, juice reserved

1 small box lemon or raspberry gelatin

1 (8-ounce) package cream cheese

1 (12-ounce) container frozen whipped topping, thawed

Combine pear and pineapple juices to equal 1 cup and bring to a boil in a small saucepan. Dissolve gelatin in juice. Transfer to a medium bowl and place in refrigerator until gelatin just begins to set, about 30–40 minutes.

In a blender, combine pears and cream cheese together until smooth. Gently blend into gelatin. Fold half of the whipped topping into gelatin mixture. Pour into a medium glass dish and chill until set. Top with remaining whipped topping.

Strawberry-Banana Sour Cream Salad

Makes **12** servings

2 small boxes strawberry-banana gelatin
2 cups boiling water
1 (16-ounce) package frozen strawberries, partially thawed
4 bananas, thinly sliced
2 cups sour cream

Dissolve gelatin in boiling water. Put half of gelatin mixture in a medium bowl and put in fridge to partially set, about 35–45 minutes. Add strawberries to remaining gelatin and stir until completely thawed. Stir in bananas. Pour gelatin with fruit into a 9 x 13-inch pan and chill until almost firm.

When gelatin in bowl is partially set, stir in sour cream. Spread mixture over set gelatin in the pan. Refrigerate until set.

Fruity Cheesecake Pudding Salad

Makes 6–8 *servings*

1 (20-ounce) can
   pineapple chunks,
   with liquid
1 small box instant
   cheesecake pudding
1 (29-ounce) can fruit
   cocktail, drained
1 (11-ounce) can
   mandarin oranges,
   drained
1 banana, sliced
1 apple, diced
Frozen whipped topping,
   thawed, optional

In a punch bowl, mix together juice from pineapple with the instant pudding. Fold fruit into pudding mixture. Top with whipped topping, if desired.

VARIATION: Try vanilla, banana, or lemon instant pudding in place of cheesecake-flavored pudding.

Island Pineapple Salad

Makes 12–14 *servings*

- 1 large box pineapple gelatin
- 3 cups boiling water
- 1 (8-ounce) can crushed pineapple
- 1 cup cold water
- 1 (8-ounce) package cream cheese, softened
- 2 cups miniature marshmallows
- 1 pint whipping cream, whipped and sweetened

In a 9 x 13-inch pan, dissolve gelatin in boiling water. Stir in pineapple with juice and cold water. Mash in cream cheese with a fork or potato masher until mostly blended. Stir in marshmallows. Chill until partially set, about 45 minutes.

Fold half the whipped cream into the partially set salad and chill until completely set. Top with remaining whipped cream before serving.

Frozen Champagne Salad

Makes 12 servings

- 1 (20-ounce) can crushed pineapple
- 1 small box strawberry-kiwi or strawberry-banana gelatin
- 1 (10-ounce) package frozen strawberries
- 1/4 cup sugar
- 1/2 cup chopped pecans or walnuts, optional
- 1 cup miniature marshmallows
- 1 (12-ounce) container frozen whipped topping, thawed

In a large bowl, mix together pineapple with juice, dry gelatin, frozen strawberries, sugar, nuts if using, marshmallows, and whipped topping. Spread in a 9 x 13-inch pan and freeze. Before serving, thaw slightly and cut into squares.

Cindy's Creamy Salad

Makes 10–12 *servings*

- 1 large box cook-and-serve vanilla pudding
- 1 large box gelatin, any flavor
- 3 cups water
- 1 (8-ounce) container frozen whipped topping, thawed
- 2 cups fresh or frozen raspberries, or 2 cups mandarin oranges, drained

Cook pudding, gelatin, and water together in a medium saucepan until it comes to a boil. Stir well and then let mixture cool. Gently fold in whipped topping and fruit of choice. Pour into a large glass bowl; chill 2–3 hours, or until completely set.

Nanny's Orange Fluff

Makes 8–10 *servings*

- 1 small box orange gelatin
- 1 (16-ounce) container cottage cheese
- 1 (11-ounce) can mandarin oranges, drained
- 1 (8-ounce) can crushed pineapple
- 1 (8-ounce) container frozen whipped topping, thawed

In a large bowl, stir dry gelatin mix into cottage cheese. Partially smash oranges with a fork and then stir into cottage cheese mixture. Add pineapple with juice. Fold in whipped topping. Transfer to a serving bowl and chill for at least 4 hours before serving.

VARIATION: Stir in 2 cups miniature marshmallows and $\frac{1}{2}$ cup chopped nuts.

Lemon Pudding Fruit Salad

Makes 14–16 *servings*

1 small box lemon
    gelatin
1½ cups boiling water
1 small box instant
    lemon or vanilla
    pudding
1 cup frozen whipped
    topping, thawed
1 (15.25-ounce) can fruit
    cocktail, drained
2 (11-ounce) cans
    mandarin oranges,
    drained
1 (8-ounce) can
    pineapple tidbits,
    drained
3 bananas, sliced

In a medium bowl, dissolve gelatin in boiling water and then refrigerate until partially set, about 1 hour. Make pudding according to package directions. Combine pudding, gelatin, and whipped topping. Fold in fruit. Transfer to a serving bowl and refrigerate until set.

Frozen Raspberry Yogurt Salad

Makes 6–8 servings

1 small box raspberry
   gelatin
1 cup boiling water
1 (6-ounce) container
   raspberry yogurt
1 cup fresh or frozen
   raspberries
1 cup frozen whipped
   topping, thawed

In a medium bowl, dissolve gelatin in boiling water. Chill until partially set, about 45 minutes. Fold in yogurt, raspberries, and whipped topping; pour into an 8 x 8-inch pan and freeze until set. Thaw slightly before serving.

Ambrosia Salad

Makes 12 servings

2 cups apricot nectar
2 small boxes orange,
   peach, or apricot
   gelatin
2 cups cold water
2 (8-ounce) cans
   crushed pineapple
2 cups frozen whipped
   topping, thawed

In a medium saucepan, bring apricot nectar to a boil. Dissolve gelatin in nectar. Stir in cold water and pineapple with juice. Chill in a 9 x 13-inch pan until partially set, about 40 minutes. Stir in whipped topping. Chill until firm.

Cherry Yogurt Salad

Makes 10–12 servings

1 small box cherry
  gelatin
1 (6-ounce) container
  cherry yogurt
1 (12-ounce) container
  frozen whipped
  topping, thawed
4 bananas, sliced*
³/₄ cup chopped
  maraschino cherries
¹/₂ cup chopped walnuts
3 cups miniature
  marshmallows

In a large bowl, stir dry gelatin into yogurt. Stir in whipped topping and mix thoroughly but gently. Fold in the bananas, cherries, walnuts, and marshmallows. Chill for at least 5 minutes before serving.

*To help prevent bananas from browning, sprinkle slices with a touch of lemon juice before stirring into salad.

Sweet Cherry Pie Salad

Makes **12** *servings*

1 large box cherry
    gelatin
2 cups boiling water
1 (20-ounce) can
    crushed pineapple
1 (20-ounce) can cherry
    pie filling
1 (8-ounce) package
    cream cheese,
    softened
1 (8-ounce) container
    sour cream
1/2 cup sugar
1 teaspoon vanilla

Dissolve gelatin in boiling water. Add pineapple with juice and pie filling and mix well. Chill until set in a 9 x 13-inch pan.

In a medium bowl, blend cream cheese, sour cream, sugar, and vanilla until smooth. Spread over set gelatin and serve.

Leafy Salads

Summer Salad

In a small bowl, combine dressing ingredients and set aside.

Combine all salad ingredients except croutons in a large bowl. When ready to serve, pour dressing over salad and toss. Sprinkle croutons over top.

Dressing
1 lemon, juiced (3–4 tablespoons)
3 cloves garlic, crushed
1 teaspoon salt
1/2 teaspoon pepper
3/4 cup light olive oil
1/4 cup sugar, or more to taste

Salad
2 small heads romaine lettuce, torn into bite-size pieces
1/2–1 pound bacon, cooked and crumbled
1 1/2–2 cups chopped tomatoes
3/4 cup sunflower seeds
1 cup grated Swiss cheese
1/3 cup grated Parmesan cheese
Croutons

Spinach Artichoke Dip Salad

Makes 6–8 *servings*

1 (6–8-ounce) bag baby spinach
1 (7.5-ounce) jar marinated artichoke hearts, drained and chopped
1½ cups Italian-blend cheese
1–1½ cups crumbled garlic cheese croutons
1 (16-ounce) bottle Hidden Valley Creamy Parmesan dressing

In a large bowl, combine the spinach, artichoke, cheese, and crouton crumbles. Gradually drizzle some of the dressing over top and toss to coat. Add more dressing to reach desired consistency.

Spinach and Mushroom Salad

Makes 10–12 servings

Dressing

1½ teaspoons poppy
   seeds
¾ cup white distilled
   vinegar
1 cup light olive oil
¾ cup sugar
1½ teaspoons salt
¾ teaspoon dry mustard

Salad

¾ pound sliced
   mushrooms
1 red onion, thinly
   sliced
1 (10-ounce) bag fresh
   spinach leaves
1 head iceberg lettuce,
   chopped
½–1 pound bacon,
   cooked and crumbled
1 cup cottage cheese
1½ cups grated Swiss
   cheese

Combine dressing ingredients in a medium bowl. Add mushrooms and onion and then cover. Refrigerate dressing 24 hours or at least overnight.

Mix all remaining salad ingredients in a large bowl. When ready to serve, pour dressing over salad and toss.

Hawaiian Honey Lemon Salad

Makes **8–10** *servings*

Honey Lemon Dressing

1/2 cup mayonnaise
1 lemon, zested and
    juiced
1 tablespoon honey
1/4 teaspoon celery salt
White pepper, to taste

Salad

1 head leafy green
    lettuce, torn into
    bite-size pieces
1 cucumber, peeled,
    sliced, and quartered
1 cup candied macada-
    mia nuts or walnuts
1 cup diced pineapple
1–2 avocados, cubed
1/2 cup real bacon
    crumbles

Combine dressing ingredients in a small bowl and mix until smooth; refrigerate until ready to use.

In a large bowl, combine the lettuce, cucumber, nuts, pineapple, and avocado. Toss with the dressing just before serving and sprinkle with bacon.

Sweet Fiesta Salad

Makes 10–12 servings

1 large head romaine lettuce, torn into bite-size pieces

1 (15-ounce) can red kidney beans, rinsed and drained

1 (15-ounce) can black beans, rinsed and drained

$\frac{1}{2}$ red onion, thinly sliced

2 cups grated cheddar cheese

1 (10-ounce) bag Fritos corn chips

1 (16-ounce) bottle Catalina dressing

In a large bowl, combine all ingredients except chips and dressing. When ready to serve, pour chips over top. Add the dressing gradually. You may not need to use it all. Toss until completely covered.

VARIATION: Add 1 tomato, diced, and $\frac{3}{4}$ cup sliced black olives.

Cranberry Mixed Greens Salad

Makes 10–12 servings

1 (10-ounce) bag spring mix salad

1 (10-ounce) bag leafy romaine salad

1 (10-ounce) bag coleslaw salad

1 (6-ounce) bag dried cranberries

1–1½ cups candied or toffee nuts

1 (12-ounce) bottle Brianna's Poppy Seed Dressing

Combine all ingredients except nuts and dressing in a large bowl. When ready to serve, sprinkle nuts over salad and pour dressing over top. Toss until completely covered.

Apple-Pear Salad

Makes 10–12 servings

Dressing

1/2 cup lemon juice
1 tablespoon Dijon
    mustard
1/2 teaspoon salt
1/4–1/2 cup sugar
2/3 cup light olive oil
1 tablespoon poppy
    seeds

Salad

2 pears, peeled and
    diced
2 Granny Smith apples,
    peeled and diced
1 large head romaine
    lettuce, torn into
    bite-size pieces
1 1/2 cups cubed sharp
    white cheddar cheese
3/4 cup dried cranberries
1 cup cashew halves

Combine dressing ingredients in a medium bowl. Add pears and apples to keep from browning, then set aside.

In a large bowl, combine remaining salad ingredients. When ready to serve, pour dressing over top and toss until completely covered.

Southwest Caesar Ensalada

Makes 4 servings

1 (10-ounce) bag Dole
  Caesar Salad kit
1 (15-ounce) can kidney
  or black beans,
  rinsed and drained
1 (8.75-ounce) can whole
  kernel corn, drained
1 medium tomato, diced
1/2 orange or yellow bell
  pepper, seeded and
  cubed
1/3–1/2 medium sweet
  onion, thinly sliced

In a large bowl, layer lettuce from the kit, beans, corn, tomato, bell pepper, and onion. Pour dressing from kit over salad. Sprinkle croutons and Parmesan from the kit over top. Cover and toss gently to coat salad with dressing. Serve immediately.

NOTE: Turn this salad into a meal by adding 1 1/2 cups grilled chicken slices.

Cherry-Swiss Salad

Makes 10–12 *servings*

Dressing

1/2 cup vegetable oil
1/2 cup cider vinegar
1/2 cup sugar
1 teaspoon dry mustard
2 teaspoons poppy seeds

Salad

2–3 tablespoons sugar
1/2 cup sliced almonds
2 (10-ounce) bags
   romaine lettuce
1 1/2 cups grated Swiss
   cheese
1 cup dried cherries,
   chopped

Combine dressing ingredients in a small bowl and set aside.

In a small frying pan, melt sugar over low to medium heat. Add almonds and stir until sugar-coated; cool and set aside. Mix all remaining salad ingredients in a large bowl. When ready to serve, pour dressing over top and toss until completely covered. Sprinkle sugared almonds over top.

Greek Salad

Makes 6–8 *servings*

1 cucumber, halved and
  then sliced
1 (4-ounce) container
  crumbled feta cheese
1/2 cup kalamata olives,
  pitted
1 cup chopped Roma
  tomatoes
1/2 red onion, thinly
  sliced
1/2 cup balsamic
  vinaigrette or Greek
  salad dressing
6 cups torn romaine
  lettuce

Toss together all ingredients except
the lettuce in a large bowl and
let chill 1–2 hours before serving.
Remove from refrigerator, toss in
lettuce, and serve. Add more dressing if necessary to coat.

Mandarin-Almond Salad

Makes 10–12 servings

Dressing
¼ cup light olive oil
3–4 tablespoons sugar
2 tablespoons vinegar
1½ teaspoons dried
   parsley
½ teaspoon salt
Pepper, to taste
Tabasco sauce, to taste

Salad
3 tablespoons sugar
½ cup sliced almonds
1 large head romaine
   lettuce
1 (11-ounce) can
   mandarin oranges,
   drained
1 small red onion, sliced
1 cup chow mein noodles
1 cup chopped celery

Combine all dressing ingredients in a small bowl and set aside.

In a small frying pan, melt sugar over low to medium heat. Add almonds and stir until sugar-coated; cool and set aside. Mix all remaining salad ingredients in a large bowl. Just before serving, pour dressing over top and toss. Sprinkle sugared almonds over top.

Pear, Gorgonzola, and Candied Pecan Salad

Makes 8 servings

1 head romaine or leafy
green lettuce, torn
into bite-size pieces
2 pears, washed and cut
into bite-size pieces*
3/4–1 cup crumbled
Gorgonzola cheese
1 cup candied pecans
3/4 cup dried cranberries
or cherries
3/4 cup real bacon
crumbles
Red wine vinaigrette

In a large bowl, layer all salad
ingredients. Just before serving,
toss with dressing, to taste.

*Toss with a little lemon juice to
prevent browning.

Ranch-Sunflower Salad

Makes **8–10** *servings*

1 head romaine lettuce,
    torn into bite-size
    pieces
1½ cups sugar snap
    peas, halved
¾ cup grated carrots
¾ cup sliced celery
1½ cups grated sharp
    cheddar cheese
3 hard-boiled eggs,
    sliced or chopped
¾–1 cup sunflower
    seeds
Ranch dressing

In a large bowl, layer the lettuce, peas, carrots, celery, cheese, and eggs. Sprinkle sunflower seeds over top. Toss just before serving, or leave layered. Serve with ranch dressing on the side.

Easy Chopped Italian Salad

Makes 6–8 *servings*

1 head romaine lettuce,
  chopped
4 ounces dry salami,
  cubed
4 ounces pepperoni,
  cubed
2 Roma tomatoes,
  chopped
2 green onions, chopped
  (green and light
  green parts only)
1½ cups grated Italian-
  blend cheese
Fresh basil, chopped
Parmesan or Caesar
  vinaigrette

Toss all ingredients together except the dressing in a large bowl. Toss with the desired amount of vinaigrette just before serving.

Bridal Shower Salad

Makes 8–10 *servings*

Dressing
1/2 cup mayonnaise
1/4 cup sugar
1/4 cup milk
1 tablespoon poppy
   seeds
2 tablespoons white or
   red wine vinegar

Salad
1 large head romaine
   lettuce, torn into
   bite-size pieces
1 pound strawberries,
   sliced
1/2 red onion, thinly
   sliced
1–1 1/2 cups halved red
   grapes

In a small bowl, combine mayonnaise, sugar, milk, poppy seeds, and vinegar; mix well and chill.

In a large bowl, combine the lettuce, strawberries, onion, and grapes. Pour dressing over top and toss just before serving.

Blue Cheese
Apple Nut Salad

Makes 4 servings

3 tablespoons olive oil
1 teaspoon Dijon
  mustard
1 teaspoon sugar
2 green onions, chopped
$1/2$ cup chopped apple
3 cups torn red leaf or
  Bibb lettuce
4 tablespoons chopped
  walnuts or pecans
4 tablespoons crumbled
  blue cheese

In a medium bowl, whisk together olive oil, mustard, and sugar. Fold onions and apple into dressing. Add lettuce and gently toss. Sprinkle nuts and blue cheese over the top. Serve immediately.

Raspberry-Chicken Salad

Makes **8–10** *servings*

2 boneless, skinless
    chicken breasts,
    cubed
Olive oil
1 tablespoon honey
1 tablespoon minced
    garlic
Salt and pepper, to taste
1 head romaine lettuce,
    torn into bite-size
    pieces
1 (10-ounce) bag spring
    mix salad
3/4 cup chopped celery
1 1/2 cups fresh
    raspberries
3/4 cup candied or toffee
    nuts
Raspberry dressing or
    vinaigrette

In a large frying pan, brown chicken in oil, honey, garlic, salt, and pepper. When done, set aside to cool.

In a large bowl, combine lettuce, spring mix salad, celery, raspberries, and nuts. Sprinkle cooled chicken over top and serve dressing on the side.

Strawberry and Blue Cheese Salad

Makes **8–10** *servings*

1 head romaine lettuce, torn into bite-size pieces

1 pound strawberries, washed and sliced

$3/4$–1 cup blue cheese crumbles

$1/2$–$3/4$ cup sliced honey-roasted almonds

Poppy seed dressing

In a large bowl, layer the lettuce, strawberries, cheese, and almonds. Just before serving, toss with the desired amount of dressing.

Candy Bar Salad

Makes 8–10 servings

Dressing

1 cup mayonnaise
1/2 cup milk
1/4 cup white vinegar
2/3 cup sugar
2 tablespoons poppy
seeds

Salad

1 pound fresh
strawberries, sliced
1 (10-ounce) bag
romaine lettuce
1 (10-ounce) bag fresh
spinach or spring
mix salad
3 Heath candy bars,
crushed

In a small bowl, combine dressing ingredients and mix well.

In a large bowl, combine salad ingredients. Pour dressing over salad just before serving and toss to coat.

Cranberry Spring Mix Salad

Makes 6–8 servings

1 (11-ounce) container spring mix salad greens
1/3 red onion, thinly sliced
1/2 cup craisins
1/3 cup chopped cilantro

Dressing

1/3 cup cranberry juice cocktail
1/3 cup balsamic vinegar
1/3 cup olive oil
1 tablespoon honey
1 teaspoon Dijon mustard
1 tablespoon finely chopped onion

In a large bowl, layer spring mix, onion, craisins, and cilantro. In a blender, puree all dressing ingredients and pour into a cruet or bottle. Refrigerate salad and dressing separately until ready to serve. Drizzle individual servings of salad with desired amount of dressing.

Strawberry-Spinach Salad with Lemon Dressing

Makes 6–8 *servings*

Lemon Dressing

2 tablespoons
   lemon zest
2 tablespoons
   lemon juice
¼ cup oil
⅓ cup sugar
1 teaspoon mustard
   seed, optional

Salad

1 cup slivered almonds,
   candied
1 (10-ounce) bag fresh
   spinach
1½ apples, peeled and
   chopped
1 cup dried cranberries
2 cups sliced
   strawberries

In a small bowl, combine dressing ingredients together and mix well.

In a large bowl, toss together salad ingredients. Pour dressing over salad just before serving and toss.

NOTE: To candy almonds, wet them and roll in sugar. Place on a baking sheet and bake at 350 degrees for 10 minutes; cool.

Berry and Orange Tossed Salad

Makes 6–8 servings

1 head romaine lettuce, torn into bite-size pieces
1 cup sliced strawberries
1 cup raspberries
1 cup blueberries
1 (11-ounce) can mandarin oranges, drained
Poppy seed dressing

Toss all ingredients together except the dressing in a large bowl. Toss with the dressing just before serving.

Simple Goat Cheese Salad

Makes 8–10 servings

1 (6-ounce) bag baby
    spinach
2 cups halved seedless
    red grapes
1 (6-ounce) container
    goat cheese, crumbled
1 cup coarsely chopped
    candied pecans*
Raspberry dressing or
    vinaigrette

Layer all salad ingredients except dressing in a large bowl. Toss with dressing just before serving or allow individuals to serve and dress their own salads.

*Walnuts and cashews can be substituted.

Lettuce Wedges

Makes 4–6 servings

1 small head iceberg
    lettuce, cut into
    4–6 wedges
3/4–1 cup blue cheese
    dressing
1/2 cup crumbled blue
    cheese
Salt and pepper, to taste
4–6 slices bacon, cooked

Place individual lettuce wedges on salad plates and evenly drizzle blue cheese dressing over top. Sprinkle with cheese, salt, and pepper. Crumble one piece of bacon over each salad wedge.

VARIATION: Other dressing and cheese combinations are Caesar and grated Asiago cheese, ranch and grated cheddar cheese, and Italian and crumbled feta cheese.

Classic Italian Salad

Makes 4 servings

1 (12-ounce) bag Dole
   American-blend
   salad
$1/3$ red onion, thinly
   sliced
25 pitted black olives
2–4 small pepperoncini*
   yellow peppers
6–8 cherry tomatoes
$1/2$ cup croutons
Italian dressing
Parmesan cheese,
   freshly grated

Place bag of salad in a large serving bowl. Layer red onion, olives, peppers, tomatoes, and croutons. Toss and serve with Italian dressing. Garnish with Parmesan cheese.

*These peppers are usually found in a jar in the condiments aisle of the grocery store.

Southwest Layered Salad

Makes 8–10 servings

1 head romaine lettuce, torn into bite-sized pieces
2 cups grated pepper jack cheese
1 (15-ounce) can black beans, rinsed and drained
1 cup frozen corn, thawed
1 large red bell pepper, diced
1 cup crushed Fritos corn chips
Ranch dressing
Salsa

In a large bowl, layer the lettuce, cheese, beans, corn, bell pepper, and chips. Combine 2 parts ranch dressing with 1 part salsa (or more if desired). Serve dressing on the side or toss just before serving.

VARIATION: For a more hearty salad, add a layer of grilled chicken cooked with a little taco seasoning or with lime juice, salt, and pepper.

Garden BLT Salad

Makes 10–12 servings

Dressing

1 cup mayonnaise
1/4 cup lemon juice
   (freshly squeezed
   or bottled)
4 teaspoons sugar
1/8 teaspoon black
   pepper
1/4 teaspoon celery salt
Dash of garlic powder
2 teaspoons granulated
   chicken bouillon

Salad

10 ounces garden rotini
   pasta, cooked and
   drained
8 slices bacon, cooked
   and crumbled
1 tomato, seeded and
   chopped
1/4 cup sliced green
   onions
1/2 cucumber, sliced and
   quartered
4 cups thinly sliced
   iceberg lettuce

Combine dressing ingredients in a small bowl and mix until smooth; refrigerate until ready to use.

In a large bowl, add salad ingredients. Toss with dressing just before serving, adding gradually to coat.

Veggie
Salads

Greek Artichoke Salad

Makes 8 servings

1 (14.75-ounce) jar
artichoke hearts,
drained and quartered

1 large cucumber,
halved and sliced

2 medium tomatoes, cut
into wedges

1 orange or yellow bell
pepper, seeded and
cubed

1 small red onion,
halved and sliced

1 (2.25-ounce) can
sliced black olives,
drained

$1/2$ cup olive oil

$1/4$ cup balsamic vinegar

2 teaspoons Italian
seasoning

1 head romaine lettuce,
washed and torn

1 (4-ounce) container
crumbled feta cheese

In a large bowl, combine artichoke hearts, cucumber, tomatoes, bell pepper, onion, and olives.

In a small bowl, whisk together olive oil, vinegar, and Italian seasoning. Drizzle dressing evenly over vegetables in the larger bowl. Cover and gently toss. Allow vegetables to marinate in the refrigerator for 30–60 minutes.

Divide romaine between 8 salad plates. Divide vegetable mixture evenly over each salad and top with crumbled feta.

Summer Garden Zucchini Salad

Makes 4–5 *servings*

5 baby zucchini, thinly
  sliced
1/2 red onion, thinly
  sliced
1 bell pepper, any color,
  seeded and cubed
2–3 fresh basil leaves,
  minced
2 tablespoons olive oil
2 tablespoons balsamic
  or apple cider vinegar
Salt and pepper, to taste

In a large bowl, combine sliced zucchini, onion, bell pepper, and basil. Drizzle olive oil and vinegar evenly over top. Cover and gently toss. Salt and pepper to taste.

Tomato and Mozzarella Salad

Makes 6–8 servings

3–4 large tomatoes, cut in ¼-inch slices
2 pounds fresh mozzarella cheese, cut in ¼-inch slices
¼ cup freshly chopped basil
Balsamic vinaigrette
Salt and pepper, to taste

Alternate tomato and mozzarella slices on a serving tray. Sprinkle with basil. Drizzle desired amount of balsamic vinaigrette over top. Sprinkle with salt and pepper.

Chilled Cucumber Salad

Makes 5–6 servings

3 cucumbers, peeled and sliced
¼ cup chopped onion
2 teaspoons dill
1 teaspoon salt
1 teaspoon sugar
½ cup balsamic vinaigrette

Place all ingredients in a medium bowl; toss well. Chill 1 hour or overnight.

VARIATION: Cucumbers can be cut in half, seeded, and cut into bite-size pieces for this recipe.

Fruity Broccoli Salad

Makes 8–10 *servings*

Dressing

1 cup mayonnaise
2 tablespoons red wine
   vinegar
$1/2$ cup sugar

Salad

5 cups broccoli florets,
   cut into bite-size
   pieces
1 cup halved red grapes
1 cup sliced or quartered
   strawberries
$1/2$–1 red onion, chopped
   or thinly sliced
1 pound bacon, cooked
   and crumbled
$2\,1/2$ cups grated sharp
   cheddar cheese
$1/2$ cup sunflower seeds

In a small bowl, combine all dressing ingredients and set aside.

In a large bowl, combine all salad ingredients. Pour dressing over top and stir. Refrigerate 1 hour before serving.

Baby Cucumber and Radish Salad

Makes 4 servings

6–8 small red radishes
3 baby cucumbers
1 yellow, orange, or red
    bell pepper
¼ cup fresh cilantro

Dressing

½ cup rice vinegar
2 ½ tablespoons sugar
2 tablespoons olive oil
¼ teaspoon cayenne
    pepper

Wash radishes. Cut off ends. Cut each in half then quarter each half. Place cut radishes in a large bowl.

Wash cucumbers, cut off ends, cut in half lengthwise, and then cut into thick slices. Add cucumber slices to bowl. Cut the stem off the bell pepper, seed, and cut the pepper into bite-size pieces and add to the bowl.

In a small bowl, whisk together vinegar, sugar, olive oil, and cayenne pepper. Chill salad and dressing separately until ready to serve.

Just before serving, toss salad, dressing, and cilantro together. Serve immediately.

Chunky Veggie Salad

Makes 10–12 *servings*

1/2 **pound baby carrots,
    halved**
1 **cucumber, peeled,
    halved, and sliced**
1 **pint grape tomatoes**
1 **cup sliced celery**
1 **small bunch radishes,
    sliced or quartered**
2 **cups sugar snap peas,
    ends trimmed**
1–2 **cups bite-size
    broccoli or
    cauliflower florets**
Ranch dressing

Mix all ingredients together in a large bowl. Serve with ranch dressing or a dressing of choice on the side.

Four-Bean Salad

Dressing
1/2 cup vinegar
1/2 cup red wine vinegar
1/2 cup light olive oil
1 cup sugar

Salad
2 (15-ounce) cans wax
  beans, drained
1 (15-ounce) can
  garbanzo beans,
  drained
2 (15-ounce) cans whole
  green beans, drained
2 (15-ounce) cans red
  kidney beans, rinsed
  and drained
1 small red onion, thinly
  sliced
1 green bell pepper,
  thinly sliced

In a small bowl, combine all dressing ingredients and set aside.

In a large bowl, combine all salad ingredients. Pour dressing over top and stir. Refrigerate 24 hours, stirring occasionally. When ready to serve, drain dressing or serve with a slotted spoon.

Ranch, Bacon, and Asparagus Salad

Makes 4 servings

1 pound fresh asparagus, trimmed

1 cup plus 1 teaspoon water

¼ cup ranch dressing

¼ cup grated Parmesan cheese

2 tablespoons real bacon bits

Place asparagus in a large frying pan and add 1 cup water; bring to a boil. Cover, reduce heat, and cook asparagus for 3–4 minutes until crisp-tender. Rinse asparagus in cold water and drain completely. Place asparagus in an airtight container and refrigerate for 1–2 hours.

Just before you are ready to serve, combine ranch dressing and 1 teaspoon water. Drizzle dressing over asparagus. Sprinkle Parmesan cheese and bacon over top. Toss to coat completely.

Cauliflower-Shrimp Salad

Makes 4 servings

Dressing
1/2 cup mayonnaise
1 teaspoon prepared
    mustard
1 tablespoon ketchup
1 tablespoon chopped
    fresh parsley
1 tablespoon chopped
    chives
1/4 teaspoon salt
Pepper, to taste

Salad
1 small head cauliflower
1/2 pound small cooked
    shrimp (or 1 can
    shrimp)

In a large bowl, combine mayonnaise, mustard, ketchup, parsley, chives, salt, and pepper.

Divide cauliflower into bite-size pieces and cook until tender in salted water.

Combine cauliflower, shrimp, and dressing mixture. Toss and refrigerate at least 30 minutes before serving.

Crunchy Pea Salad

Makes 8–10 *servings*

2 cups frozen peas, thawed

¾ cup sliced or diced celery

2 cups bite-size cauliflower florets

¼ cup sliced green onions

½ cup sliced fresh mushrooms

1 cup cashews

1½ cups grated cheddar cheese

8–10 slices bacon, cooked and crumbled

½–1 cup ranch dressing

In a large bowl, combine all ingredients. Add more dressing, if needed. Sprinkle additional green onions and bacon over top as garnish, if desired.

Bacon Broccoli Salad

Makes 6–8 *servings*

**6 cups fresh broccoli,
coarsely chopped**
²/₃ cup real bacon bits*
**2 cups grated sharp
cheddar cheese**
**½ large red onion,
chopped**

Dressing
**¼ cup apple cider
vinegar**
2 tablespoons sugar
1 teaspoon black pepper
½ teaspoon salt
²/₃ cup mayonnaise
1 teaspoon lemon juice

In a large bowl, toss together broccoli, bacon, cheese, and onion.

In a small bowl, combine vinegar, sugar, pepper, salt, mayonnaise, and lemon juice.

Mix dressing into salad. Cover and refrigerate until ready to serve.

VARIATIONS: Add ²/₃ cup raisins or craisins to salad.

*Substitute 10–12 slices of bacon, cooked and crumbled, in place of real bacon bits, if desired.

Mexicorn Bean Salad

Makes 6–8 *servings*

Dressing

3 tablespoons olive oil
3 tablespoons vinegar
1 tablespoon dry ranch
   dressing mix

Salad

1 (16-ounce) can kidney
   beans, rinsed and
   drained
1 (15-ounce) can black
   beans, rinsed and
   drained
1 (11-ounce) can
   Mexicorn, drained
¼ cup sliced green
   onions

In a large bowl, mix oil, vinegar, and ranch dressing mix together until powder is thoroughly dissolved.

Fold beans, corn, and onions into dressing until evenly coated. Cover and refrigerate until ready to serve.

Avocado Salad

Makes 6 servings

2 large avocados
$1/2$–1 red onion, chopped
$1/2$–1 red bell pepper,
  chopped
2 small tomatoes,
  chopped
$1/4$ cup chopped fresh
  cilantro
1 small lime, juiced
Salt and pepper, to taste

Peel, pit, and dice avocados. In a medium bowl, combine avocados, onion, bell pepper, tomatoes, cilantro, and lime juice. Gently toss to coat veggies in juice. Add salt and pepper, to taste.

Ensalada Chilena

Makes 8–10 servings

1 medium red onion,
  julienned
5 medium tomatoes,
  sliced
Olive or vegetable oil,
  to taste
2 tablespoons chopped
  cilantro
Salt, to taste

Place cut onion in a large bowl and cover with water 2–3 hours to soften; drain. Stir together tomato slices and onion. Lightly drizzle oil over mixture. Sprinkle with cilantro and salt; stir again. Serve immediately or chill until ready to serve.

NOTE: Onions can soak all day.

Cashew Broccoli Slaw

Makes 6 servings

Dressing

1 cup plain yogurt*
¹⁄₃ cup sugar
1 tablespoon apple cider vinegar

Salad

1 (12-ounce) bag broccoli coleslaw
¹⁄₄ cup chopped green onions
1 cup raisins or craisins
1 cup cashew pieces

In a medium bowl, whisk together yogurt, sugar, and vinegar until smooth.

Add coleslaw, green onions, and raisins or craisins to the bowl. Fold slaw mixture into dressing until evenly coated. Chill until ready to serve. Toss cashews into the salad right before serving.

*Mayonnaise or Miracle Whip can be used in place of yogurt.

Bell Pepper Salad

Makes 6–8 *servings*

1 red bell pepper, diced
1 yellow or orange bell
    pepper, diced
1 green bell pepper,
    diced
1/2 cup chopped red
    onion
1/4 cup chopped fresh
    parsley
1/2 cup balsamic
    vinaigrette

Combine all ingredients in a medium bowl. Cover and chill until ready to serve.

Cauliflower–Green Pea Salad

Makes 8–10 *servings*

1 head cauliflower
1 (16-ounce) bag frozen
    peas, thawed

Dressing

1 cup sour cream
1/3 cup mayonnaise
1 envelope ranch
    dressing mix

Clean and cut cauliflower into bite-size pieces. Combine cauliflower and peas in a large bowl.

In a small bowl, combine sour cream, mayonnaise, and ranch dressing mix.

Toss cauliflower and peas together with dressing mixture. Chill until ready to serve.

Ranch Cauliflower and Broccoli Salad

Makes 6–8 servings

1 medium head
    cauliflower
$1/2$ medium head broccoli
$1/3$ cup sliced green
    onions
1 red or yellow bell
    pepper, diced
$1/2$ cup raisins

Dressing

1 envelope ranch
    dressing mix
1 cup mayonnaise
1 cup plain yogurt

Clean and cut vegetables into bite-size pieces. Place vegetables and raisins in a large bowl.

Combine ranch seasoning, mayonnaise, and yogurt in a small bowl. Stir ranch mixture into vegetables until evenly covered. Refrigerate until ready to serve.

Pasta Salads

Jenny's Cashew Bow-Tie Pasta

Makes **8–10** *servings*

12 ounces bow-tie
   pasta, cooked and
   cooled
$1/2$–1 pound chicken,
   cooked and cubed*
1 cup sliced celery
$1^1/4$ cups ranch
   dressing**
$1/2$ teaspoon salt
$1/2$ cup sautéed
   mushroom slices
$1/4$ cup chopped green
   onions
1 cup frozen peas,
   thawed
1 cup cashews

Mix pasta, chicken, celery, ranch dressing, and salt in a large bowl. Refrigerate 5 hours. Stir in mushrooms, onions, and peas. Sprinkle with cashews and serve. Add more dressing, if necessary.

*Sauté chicken in light olive oil, salt, and pepper.

**Ranch dressing made from a dry mix tastes best here.

Ham, Swiss, and Artichoke Pasta Salad

Makes 6–8 *servings*

1 (14.5-ounce) jar marinated artichoke hearts

2 cups cubed ham

4–6 ounces Swiss cheese, cubed

3/4 cup minced fresh parsley

10–12 ounces rotini pasta, cooked and cooled

1½ tablespoons Dijon mustard

1/3 cup olive oil

Salt and pepper, to taste

Drain the artichoke hearts and reserve about 1/2 cup of the marinade; cut hearts into quarters.

In a large bowl, toss together the artichoke hearts, ham, cheese, parsley, and pasta.

Combine reserved marinade, mustard, and olive oil. Toss with salad ingredients and then season with salt and pepper. Chill until ready to serve.

Perfect Picnic Pasta Salad

Makes 8–10 servings

16 ounces rotini pasta,
  cooked and cooled
1½ cups bite-size
  broccoli florets
1 red bell pepper, diced
1 green bell pepper,
  diced
8 ounces medium
  or sharp cheddar
  cheese, cubed
1 (4-ounce) can sliced
  black olives, drained
½ small onion, finely
  chopped
1–1½ cups Italian
  dressing

Mix all ingredients together in a large bowl. Refrigerate 1–2 hours before serving. Add more dressing, if necessary.

Feta Pasta Salad

Makes 8 servings

**12 ounces penne or
rotini pasta, cooked
and cooled**

**1 orange bell pepper,
diced**

1 red bell pepper, diced

**½–1 cup chopped sun-
dried tomatoes**

**2 cups firmly packed
fresh baby spinach**

**1 (4-ounce) container
crumbled feta cheese**

**1–1½ cups Caesar
dressing**

Gently combine all ingredients
in a large bowl until coated with
dressing. Refrigerate until ready to
serve, and add more dressing to
moisten, if necessary.

Chicken Caesar Pasta Salad

Makes 8–10 *servings*

- 12–16 ounces bow-tie pasta, cooked and cooled
- 8–10 boneless, skinless chicken tenders, cooked and cubed
- 3–4 cups fresh spinach leaves
- 1½ cups frozen peas, thawed
- 1½ cups Caesar dressing
- Salt and pepper, to taste
- ½ cup grated Asiago cheese

Mix together all ingredients in a large bowl. Refrigerate 1–2 hours before serving. Add more dressing, if necessary.

Salmon Macaroni Salad

Makes 4–6 servings

1 tablespoon minced
  onion
1 teaspoon dried
  cilantro
$3/4$ cup mayonnaise
$1/4$ teaspoon salt
$1/4$ teaspoon pepper
2 cups uncooked
  macaroni, cooked
  and cooled
1 cup cubed cucumber
1 cup cubed cheddar
  cheese
1 (7.5-ounce) can salmon,
  drained and flaked

In a medium bowl, combine the
onion, cilantro, mayonnaise, salt,
and pepper. Fold in macaroni,
cucumber, cheese, and salmon
until coated. Refrigerate until
ready to serve.

Shrimp and Seashell Salad

Makes **8–10** servings

- 12 ounces small shell pasta, cooked and cooled
- 2–3 stalks celery, diced
- 2 (4-ounce) cans tiny shrimp, drained
- 1 small onion, finely chopped
- 1–1½ cups Miracle Whip

Mix all ingredients together in a large bowl. Refrigerate 1–2 hours. Add more Miracle Whip before serving, if necessary.

Tuna Noodle Pasta Salad

Makes **8–10** servings,

- 12 ounces rotini pasta, cooked and cooled
- 1 (12-ounce) can white tuna, drained
- 1 cup diced celery
- 1 (16-ounce) bag frozen peas, thawed
- 1 head lettuce, shredded
- 1 cup mayonnaise
- ¼ cup milk
- Salt and pepper, to taste

Combine the pasta, tuna, celery, peas, and lettuce in a large bowl.

In a small bowl, mix mayonnaise with enough milk to slightly thin it out. Pour over pasta salad mixture and stir until completely covered. Season with salt and pepper.

Classic Macaroni Salad

Makes 8–10 *servings*

**12–16 ounces small
shell pasta, cooked
and cooled**
1 cup chopped celery
**¼ cup finely chopped
onion**
**1 (16-ounce) package
frozen peas and
carrots, thawed**
**4 hard-boiled eggs,
slightly chopped***
¾ cup Miracle Whip
½ teaspoon salt
**½ teaspoon pepper
paprika**

Combine all ingredients except
paprika in a large bowl. Refrigerate 1–2 hours before serving. Add
more Miracle Whip, if needed.
Sprinkle paprika over top for
colorful garnish.

*Slice one egg for decorative
garnish on top of salad and then
sprinkle with paprika.

Grilled Veggie Pasta Salad

Makes **8–10** *servings*

Olive oil
Salt and pepper, to taste
1 zucchini, sliced
1 yellow squash, sliced
1 yellow or red onion,
sliced into rings
1 red bell pepper, sliced
1 green bell pepper,
sliced
16 ounces spaghetti
noodles, broken
into thirds, cooked,
drained, and cooled
¹/₂–1 cup grated Asiago
and/or Parmesan
cheese

Brush a grill pan with olive oil and heat. Place vegetable slices in the pan and season with salt and pepper; grill until slightly browned and tender. Set aside to cool. When cool, cut veggies into bite-size pieces.

In a large bowl, toss grilled vegetables with pasta and cheese; drizzle with a little olive oil and toss again. Top with more cheese and salt and pepper, to taste. Serve chilled.

Southwest Pasta Salad

Makes 8–10 *servings*

- **12–16 ounces rotini pasta, cooked and cooled**
- **1 red bell pepper, diced**
- **1 yellow bell pepper, diced**
- **1 (15-ounce) can black beans, rinsed and drained**
- **1 cup frozen kernel corn, thawed**
- **$^{1}/_{2}$ head iceberg lettuce, chopped**
- **1 cup cubed pepper jack cheese**
- **$^{1}/_{2}$ cup pepitas, optional**
- **1 (16-ounce) bottle Hidden Valley Southwest Chipotle Salad Dressing**

In a large bowl, combine all ingredients except dressing. Toss with half the dressing and chill 1 hour. Gradually add remaining dressing to desired consistency just before serving.

VARIATION: Chopped onion and cilantro are also great additions to this salad.

Orzo Salad with Feta

Makes 4–6 servings

1 cup uncooked orzo
   pasta
1/2 cup sliced green
   olives
1 cup crumbled feta
   cheese
1/4 cup chopped fresh
   parsley
6–8 cherry tomatoes,
   halved or quartered*
1 yellow bell pepper,
   seeded and chopped
1 cup Greek vinaigrette
   (or other favorite
   vinaigrette)

Cook the orzo according to package directions; rinse and drain. When cool, combine the orzo in a large bowl with the olives, cheese, parsley, tomatoes, and bell pepper. Toss with the dressing and serve.

*Substitute 1/2 cup chopped roasted red pepper, or more, if desired.

Fruity Bow-Tie Pasta Salad

Makes 10–12 servings

16 ounces bow-tie pasta, cooked and cooled

1 cup craisins

2 cups red grapes, halved

1 (11-ounce) can mandarin oranges, drained

1 (8-ounce) can pineapple tidbits, drained

³/₄ cup cashew pieces

2 green onions, chopped

1 cup diced celery

Dressing

1 cup coleslaw dressing

¹/₂ cup mayonnaise

In a large bowl, combine pasta, craisins, grapes, oranges, pineapple, cashews, onions, and celery.

In a small bowl, combine coleslaw dressing and mayonnaise. Drizzle dressing over salad, and gently toss.

Angie's Balsamic Chicken Pasta Salad

Makes **8–10** *servings*

1 pint grape tomatoes, halved

3 tablespoons chopped cilantro

1 cup sliced or coarsely chopped zucchini

2–3 cups bite-size broccoli florets

1 (4-ounce) can sliced black olives

1/2 cup chopped onion

1 (16-ounce) bottle balsamic vinaigrette dressing, divided

3 boneless, skinless chicken breasts, cut into bite-size pieces

12 ounces bow-tie pasta, cooked and cooled

3 cups fresh spinach

1 cup crumbled fresh feta cheese*

Place tomatoes cilantro, zucchini, broccoli, olives, and onion in a large bowl. Pour about half the balsamic vinaigrette over top and stir. Marinate for 1 hour in the refrigerator.

Preheat oven to 350 degrees. Bake chicken pieces brushed with a little of the reserved balsamic vinaigrette, for 20–25 minutes, or until done.

Add the cooked chicken, pasta, spinach, and cheese to the vegetable mixture. Use remaining balsamic vinaigrette dressing to moisten pasta to desired consistency.

*Asiago or Parmesan cheese may be substituted.

Chunky Chicken Pasta Salad

Makes 8–10 servings

2 cups uncooked large
   shell pasta, cooked
   and cooled
3 chicken breasts,
   cooked and cubed
1 (8-ounce) can
   pineapple tidbits,
   drained
1 cup chopped unpeeled
   Gala apples
1 cup halved seedless
   red grapes
1 cup diced celery
2 tablespoons finely
   chopped onion
1 cup cashews
Salt and pepper, to taste

Dressing
1/2 cup coleslaw
   dressing
1/2 cup mayonnaise

Combine cooked pasta, chicken, fruit, celery, onion, and cashews in a large bowl.

In a small bowl, mix dressing and mayonnaise. Stir into salad mixture. Add more dressing, if desired. Season with salt and pepper.

VARIATION: You can use 1 cup coleslaw dressing and eliminate the mayonnaise.

Heart-Loving Pasta Salad

3 cups uncooked fusilli or rotini pasta

1 cup broccoli florets

1 cup cauliflower florets

1/2 cup chopped red onion

1/2 cup thinly sliced carrots

1 red or orange bell pepper, seeded and cubed

Dressing

3/4 cup light mayonnaise

1/4 cup vinegar

2 tablespoons white sugar or Splenda

Cook pasta according to package directions. While pasta is cooking, combine broccoli, cauliflower, onion, carrots, and bell pepper in a large serving bowl.

Drain and rinse pasta under cold water. Add pasta to bowl of vegetables; gently toss to combine.

In a small bowl, whisk the mayonnaise, vinegar, and sugar together until smooth. Pour dressing over salad and fold vegetable pasta mixture into dressing until coated. Refrigerate until ready to serve.

Ranch Shell Pasta Salad

Makes 10–12 servings

**1 envelope ranch
  dressing mix**
1/2 cup milk
3/4 cup mayonnaise
**16 ounces small shell
  pasta, cooked and
  cooled**
**1 (16-ounce) bag frozen
  peas, thawed and
  drained**
**1/3 cup sliced green
  onions**

In a large bowl, combine dressing mix, milk, and mayonnaise. Gently combine pasta, peas, and green onions with ranch mixture. Chill until ready to serve.

Bacon Ranch Pasta Salad

Makes 8–10 servings

**12–16 ounces rotini
  pasta, cooked and
  cooled**
**2 1/2 cups chopped
  cooked chicken**
1/2 cup real bacon bits
1 1/2 cups ranch dressing
**2 1/2 cups bite-size
  broccoli florets**
**1 1/2 cups grated medium
  cheddar cheese**
1/3 cup sunflower seeds

Mix all ingredients together in a large bowl and chill. Add more dressing, if necessary, before serving.

Red Potato–Pasta Salad

Makes 10–12 servings

6 red potatoes, diced

12–16 ounces rotini pasta, cooked and cooled

1 yellow bell pepper, seeded and diced

1/2 cup sliced green onions

1/2 cup mayonnaise

1 cup ranch dressing

3/4 cup real bacon bits

In a medium saucepan, cover potatoes with water and bring to a boil over high heat. Reduce to medium-low heat and simmer 10–15 minutes or until tender. Drain and rinse potatoes with cold water.

Place pasta and potatoes in a large bowl; stir in bell pepper, green onions, mayonnaise, and ranch dressing. Refrigerate until ready to serve. Stir in bacon bits just before serving.

Pizza Pasta Salad

Makes 8–10 servings

12 ounces penne pasta, cooked and cooled

30 slices pepperoni, halved

1 1/2–2 cups mozzarella cheese, cubed

1 cup sliced green olives

1 green bell pepper, diced

1 cup sliced mushrooms

1 cup Italian dressing

1/4 cup grated Parmesan cheese

Combine all ingredients except Parmesan in a large bowl. Once combined, sprinkle Parmesan as a garnish over top. Refrigerate 1–2 hours before serving. Add more dressing, if necessary.

Summer Feta Pasta Salad

Makes 4–6 servings

1/2 large red bell pepper
1/2 large green bell pepper
10–12 cherry or grape tomatoes
8 ounces rotini pasta, cooked and cooled
1 (10–13-ounce) can chicken breast meat, drained
3/4 cup Caesar dressing
1/3 cup crumbled feta cheese

Cut bell peppers into small bite-size pieces. Place tomatoes and peppers into a medium bowl. Add pasta, chicken, and dressing. Gently stir to combine all ingredients. Sprinkle feta cheese over top. Refrigerate until ready to serve.

Lemon Tarragon Chicken Pasta Salad

Makes 6–8 servings

Lemon Tarragon Dressing

1/2 cup olive oil mayonnaise
1 lemon, zested and juiced
1 tablespoon minced or grated shallot
1 heaping tablespoon chopped fresh tarragon, or 1 teaspoon dried tarragon
Dash of salt and paprika

Salad

3 cups uncooked large shell pasta, cooked and drained
2 chicken breasts, cooked and cubed
1 cup sliced celery
1 cup cashew pieces
1/2 cup sliced green onions
1 1/2 cups halved seedless red grapes

In a small bowl, combine the dressing ingredients and refrigerate until ready to use.

In a large bowl, combine the cooled cooked pasta, chicken, celery, cashews, onions, and grapes. Toss with the dressing and refrigerate for 30 minutes before serving.

Tangy Tricolor Pasta Salad

Makes 10–15 *servings*

Dressing

1¼ cups sugar
½ cup vinegar
1 tablespoon ground
  mustard
1 teaspoon garlic
  powder
½ teaspoon salt

Salad

16 ounces tricolor rotini
  pasta, cooked and
  cooled
½ cup chopped red
  onion
2 large tomatoes,
  chopped
1 large cucumber,
  peeled and cubed

In a small saucepan, heat sugar, vinegar, mustard, garlic powder, and salt together over low heat until sugar dissolves to make dressing.

In a large bowl, combine cooked pasta, onion, tomatoes, and cucumber.

Pour dressing over pasta mixture and toss to coat. Chill for 2 hours or overnight. Toss again before serving.

VARIATION: A green bell pepper, seeded and diced, or chopped cooked ham can be added to this salad.

Primavera Pasta Salad

Makes 8–10 servings

16 ounces bow-tie
  pasta, cooked and
  cooled
4 Roma tomatoes, diced
4 green onions, thinly
  sliced
1 (4-ounce) can sliced
  black olives
1 (3-ounce) jar green
  olives, sliced
1 (14-ounce) can
  quartered artichoke
  hearts, halved
1 cup chopped fresh
  Italian parsley
2 teaspoons dried basil
1/4 cup olive oil
1 (12-ounce) bottle
  Italian dressing,
  divided
1 cup pine nuts
1–2 cups grated
  Parmesan cheese
Pepper, to taste

In a large bowl, combine pasta, tomatoes, onions, olives, artichoke hearts, parsley, basil, olive oil, and half the Italian dressing, chill overnight. Before serving, add remaining dressing to desired consistency. Stir in pine nuts, cheese, and pepper.

Turkey Club Pasta Salad

Makes 6–8 servings

10–12 ounces radiatore pasta, cooked according to directions

2 cups cubed turkey breast

1/2 cup real bacon crumbles

1–2 Roma tomatoes, chopped

1 heaping cup sharp cheddar cheese cubes

3 cups shredded iceberg lettuce

1 cup ranch dressing, plus more if necessary

Combine all of the salad ingredients in a large bowl and refrigerate 1–2 hours before serving. If salad seems a little dry, stir in more dressing to moisten.

Barbecue &
Picnic Salads

Three-Cheese Potato Salad

Makes 8–10 *servings*

Dressing
1 cup mayonnaise
1 cup sour cream
1 tablespoon mustard
¼ cup milk

Salad
3–3½ pounds red or
    new potatoes, boiled
    and cubed
4 green onions, thinly
    sliced (green part
    only)
1 pound bacon, cooked
    and crumbled
4 ounces sharp cheddar
    cheese, cubed
4 ounces Monterey Jack
    cheese, cubed
4 ounces Swiss or
    Gruyère cheese,
    cubed
Salt and pepper, to taste

In a small bowl, combine the mayonnaise, sour cream, mustard, and milk.

In a large bowl, combine the potatoes and green onions. Spoon dressing over potato mixture and gently stir until completely covered. Stir in bacon and cheeses and season with salt and pepper to taste. Chill until ready to serve. Garnish with more green onions and bacon, if desired.

Mom's Potato Salad

Makes 8–10 *servings*

3–3½ pounds red potatoes, boiled and cubed

4–5 hard-boiled eggs, sliced

½ cup diced dill pickles

½ cup finely chopped onion, optional

Salt and pepper, to taste

Dressing

1 cup mayonnaise

1 cup sour cream

1 tablespoon mustard

¼ cup milk

Mix together the potatoes, eggs, pickles, and onion, if desired, in a large bowl and set aside.

In a medium bowl, combine mayonnaise, sour cream, mustard, and milk until smooth.

Spoon dressing over potato mixture and gently stir until completely covered. Season with salt and pepper.

Bacon Ranch Potato Salad

Makes 10–12 servings

15–16 medium red potatoes*

2 cups mayonnaise

1/2 cup chopped green onion

1 envelope ranch dressing mix

1 pound bacon, cooked and crumbled

Place potatoes in a large pot and cover with water. Boil 20–25 minutes, or until tender. Drain and then run cold water over potatoes. Once potatoes are cooled, cut into cubes.

In a large bowl, combine mayonnaise, green onion, and ranch mix. Gently stir in potatoes. Cover and refrigerate at least 3 hours. Just before serving, stir in bacon.

*Approximately 5 pounds of potatoes.

German Potato Salad

Makes 6–8 *servings*

- 6–8 large red potatoes
- 1–2 bouillon cubes, boiled in 1½ cups water
- 1 tablespoon Maggi seasoning*
- ⅛ cup white vinegar
- ⅛ cup dill pickle juice
- ¼ medium onion, finely chopped, optional
- ½ cup vegetable oil
- 1 teaspoon salt
- 1 teaspoon pepper
- 3 tablespoons chopped parsley
- 3 slices pastrami, chopped
- ½ cup chopped dill pickles

Boil potatoes in their skins until fork tender. Peel and allow to cool a little. Slice, place in a large bowl, and add all remaining ingredients except pastrami and dill pickles to potatoes; mix well. The salad should be quite moist. Taste and adjust seasoning. Sprinkle pastrami and pickles over top for garnish. Can be eaten cold or warm.

*Available at most large chain grocery stores.

Baked Potato Salad

Makes 6–8 servings

Dressing

1 cup mayonnaise
1 cup sour cream
1 tablespoon mustard
¼ cup milk

Salad

6 red or new potatoes,
    boiled and cubed
½ cup finely chopped
    onion
Salt and pepper, to taste
1 pound bacon, cooked
    and crumbled
2 cups grated cheddar
    cheese
Chives, chopped

In a small bowl, combine mayonnaise, sour cream, mustard, and milk until smooth; set aside.

Mix potatoes and onion together in a medium bowl. Spoon dressing over potato mixture and gently stir until completely covered. Season with salt and pepper. Just before serving, layer bacon and cheese over top. Garnish with chives.

Gorgonzola Potato Salad

Makes 6–8 *servings*

2½–3 pounds red potatoes, cut into bite-size pieces

⅓ cup olive oil

3 tablespoons red wine or apple cider vinegar

1 tablespoon Dijon mustard

1 bunch chives or 3–4 green onions, chopped

1 (5-ounce) container crumbled Gorgonzola cheese

½ pound bacon, cooked and crumbled

Salt and pepper, to taste

Boil potato pieces in salted water until tender, about 12–15 minutes; drain and cool completely.

In a large bowl, whisk together the oil, vinegar, and mustard until smooth. Add the cooled potatoes, chives, cheese, and bacon. Toss gently to coat. Season with salt and pepper and serve.

Sweet Potato Salad

Makes **8–10** *servings*

2 pounds sweet potatoes, peeled and cubed
1/2 cup mayonnaise
1/4 cup firmly packed brown sugar
1/4 teaspoon salt
1 cup roughly chopped candied pecans
1/3–1/2 cup sliced green onions

Boil the potatoes in a large pot until tender, about 8–10 minutes, depending on size of potato cubes; drain and let cool.

In a large bowl, combine mayonnaise, brown sugar, and salt. Stir in the potatoes, nuts, and green onions. Chill for 1–2 hours before serving.

VARIATION: Replace the candied pecans with salted cashews for a different taste.

Chicken and Grape Salad

Makes **8–10** *servings*

5–6 cups cooked and cubed chicken
1–1½ cups halved seedless red grapes
3/4–1 cup chopped celery
1/2 cup slivered almonds or cashew halves
1–1½ cups mayonnaise
Salt and pepper, to taste
Large lettuce leaves or croissants

Mix chicken, grapes, celery, and nuts together in a large bowl. Stir in mayonnaise gradually to desired consistency. Season with salt and pepper. When ready to serve, scoop individual servings onto large lettuce leaves or in a croissant.

Feta and Dill Chicken Salad

Makes 6 servings

3 cups diced cooked
   chicken
2 large stalks celery,
   diced
1 red bell pepper,
   seeded and cubed
1/2 red onion, diced

Dressing

1/3 cup mayonnaise
1/2 cup plain yogurt
1 (4-ounce) container
   crumbled feta cheese
2 teaspoons dried dill
   weed

In a medium bowl, combine the chicken, celery, bell pepper, and onion.

In a small bowl, combine mayonnaise, yogurt, cheese, and dill.

Spoon mayonnaise mixture over chicken mixture. Stir until chicken is completely coated. Refrigerate until ready to serve. Serve over a bed of lettuce or in pitas or croissants.

Curry Chicken Salad

Dressing
1/3 cup mayonnaise
1/2 teaspoon curry
    powder
Dash paprika
Dash salt

Salad
1 large chicken breast,
    cooked and cubed
1/2 cup slivered almonds
1/2 cup diced celery
1 cup halved seedless
    red grapes
3/4 cup shredded or
    matchstick carrots
1 green onion, sliced

In a small bowl, combine the mayonnaise, curry powder, paprika, and salt; set aside.

In a large bowl, combine the salad ingredients and then stir in the dressing mixture. Let chill 30 minutes and then serve. Great wrapped in large lettuce leaves, tortillas, or as a filling for croissant sandwiches.

Craisin Chicken Salad

Makes 6–8 servings

- 1 cup mayonnaise
- 1 teaspoon paprika
- 1/2 teaspoon seasoned salt
- 1 1/2 cups craisins
- 1 cup chopped apple
- 3 green onions, chopped
- 1/2 cup diced green bell pepper
- 1 cup chopped pecans
- 4 cups shredded cooked chicken

In a large bowl, stir together mayonnaise, paprika, and seasoned salt. Stir in craisins, apple, onions, bell pepper, and nuts. Fold in chicken until completely coated. Chill 1 hour or more before serving.

VARIATION: This salad is great when served as a filling for croissant sandwiches. Makes 12 sandwiches.

Turkey and Apple Salad

Makes 2–3 servings

1 (5-ounce) can turkey, drained*
¹⁄₂ cup diced apple
¹⁄₄ cup diced celery
¹⁄₄ cup Miracle Whip or mayonnaise

Stir all ingredients together in a medium bowl. Cover and chill for 2–3 hours before serving. Serve on croissants or over bed of lettuce.

*Leftover cooked turkey can also be used in this recipe.

Black Bean Mango Salad

Makes 6 servings

2 ripe mangos, peeled and diced
¹⁄₂ cup Italian dressing
2 bell peppers, any color, chopped
2 (15-ounce) cans black beans, rinsed and drained
¹⁄₂ cup chopped red onion
Salt and pepper, to taste

In a blender, blend ¼ cup diced mango with Italian dressing until smooth. Set aside.

In a large bowl, combine bell peppers, beans, onion, and remaining mango. Pour dressing mixture evenly over top. Cover bowl and gently toss salad. Season with salt and pepper, to taste. Refrigerate until ready to serve.

Egg Salad with Bacon

Makes 4 servings

1/2 cup chopped celery

1/3 cup mayonnaise

2–3 teaspoons prepared
   mustard

1/4–1/2 teaspoon Tabasco
   sauce

8 hard-boiled eggs,
   chopped

Salt and pepper, to taste

5 slices bacon, cooked
   and crumbled

8 slices bread

In a medium bowl, combine all ingredients except bacon. Add bacon to mixture just before serving. Evenly divide egg mixture and spoon over 4 slices of bread. Cover with remaining slices.

VARIATION: Add sliced Monterey Jack cheese and lettuce to make a more filling sandwich.

Ranch Cornbread Salad

Makes 12–15 servings

Dressing

1¼ cups sour cream
1½ cups mayonnaise
1 envelope ranch
    dressing mix

Salad

1 (15-ounce) box
    cornbread mix
2 (15-ounce) cans red
    kidney beans, rinsed
    and drained
3 medium tomatoes,
    chopped
2 cups grated sharp
    cheddar cheese
2 (11-ounce) cans
    Mexican-style corn,
    drained
½ cup chopped green
    onion
1 cup real bacon bits

In a small bowl, whisk together sour cream, mayonnaise, and ranch dressing mix; refrigerate until ready to use.

Prepare and bake cornbread in an 8 x 8-inch pan according to the directions on the box. Allow cornbread to cool completely.

Crumble ½ the cornbread in the bottom of a large glass bowl. Layer half of each of the following ingredients: beans, tomatoes, cheese, corn, and green onion. Spread half the ranch dressing mixture over top. Repeat the layers with the remaining ingredients. Top with remaining ranch dressing mixture. Cover and chill for at least 2 hours. Sprinkle bacon bits over top just before serving.

VARIATION: Add 1 (4-ounce) can green chiles and 1 teaspoon cumin to the cornbread batter before baking for a Southwest flavor.

Oriental Cashew Coleslaw

Makes 6–8 *servings*

1 (3-ounce) package oriental ramen noodles with seasoning packet
1 (16-ounce) bag coleslaw salad
1/3 cup cashew pieces
1/4 cup sliced green onions

Dressing

1/2 cup olive or canola oil
1/3 cup apple cider or rice vinegar
3 tablespoons sugar
Ramen seasoning packet

Crush noodles into small pieces, reserving seasoning packet for dressing.

In a large bowl, toss crushed noodles, coleslaw, cashews, and onions.

In a small bowl, combine oil, vinegar, sugar, and seasoning packet. Pour dressing over coleslaw mixture and toss to coat. Serve immediately.

Sweet Slaw Salad

Dressing

¼ cup vegetable oil
1 large lemon, zested
    and juiced
2 tablespoons honey
1–2 tablespoons vinegar
Salt and pepper, to taste
Dash of nutmeg
1 teaspoon poppy seeds

Salad

1 (14-ounce) bag
    coleslaw salad mix
2 small apples, chopped
1 cup chopped celery
2 green onions, sliced
    (green and light
    green parts only)
½ cup sunflower seeds

Combine the dressing ingredients in a small bowl and set aside.

Combine all the salad ingredients in a large bowl and pour dressing over top; mix well. Refrigerate at least 2 hours before serving.

Hawaiian Coleslaw

Makes 6–8 servings

3/4 cup mayonnaise
2 tablespoons vinegar
2 tablespoons sugar
1–2 tablespoons milk
4 cups shredded
    cabbage
3/4 cup shredded carrots
1 (8-ounce) can
    pineapple tidbits,
    drained
Paprika, optional

In a small bowl, combine mayonnaise, vinegar, sugar, and milk; set aside.

In a large bowl, combine cabbage, carrots, and pineapple. Pour dressing on top and stir to coat. Sprinkle paprika over top, if desired, and then refrigerate 1–2 hours before serving.

Easy Crab Salad

Makes 2 servings

1/2 cup diced green bell
    pepper
1/2 cup chopped onion
2 tablespoons butter
1 (6-ounce) can
    crabmeat, drained
1/2 cup mayonnaise
Paprika

Sauté bell pepper and onion in butter for 3–4 minutes until vegetables soften. Stir in crabmeat and sauté an additional 3 minutes. Remove from heat and stir in mayonnaise. Serve hot or cover and chill for 2 hours or overnight before serving. Serve on croissants or over bed of lettuce. Sprinkle with paprika, to garnish.

Veggie Salad Pizza

Makes 12 servings

2 (8-ounce) cans refrig-
erated crescent roll
dough

2 (8-ounce) packages
cream cheese,
softened

1 cup plain yogurt

1 envelope ranch
dressing mix

1 cup chopped fresh
broccoli

1 cup cherry tomatoes,
halved

1 cup cubed cucumber

1 orange or yellow bell
pepper, seeded and
cubed

1 cup shredded carrots

1/2 cup chopped green
onion

1 cup grated cheddar
cheese

Preheat oven to 375 degrees.

Roll the crescent roll dough onto the bottom of a 9 x 13-inch pan prepared with nonstick cooking spray. Press edges together to form crust. Bake for 12 minutes or until lightly golden brown. Allow crust to cool completely.

In a small bowl, mix together cream cheese, yogurt, and ranch dressing mix until smooth. Spread the cream cheese mixture evenly over cooled crust. Arrange vege-tables evenly over the top. Sprinkle cheese over top. Chill until ready to serve.

Fruit Salad Pizza

Makes 15 *servings*

1 white cake mix
1 egg
$^1/_2$ cup butter or
   margarine, melted
$^1/_2$ cup flour
$^1/_4$ cup powdered sugar
1 (8-ounce) container
   cream cheese,
   softened
1 (8-ounce) container
   frozen whipped
   topping, thawed
Sliced strawberries,
   bananas, kiwifruit,
   pineapple, apples,
   blueberries, peaches,
   and grapes
1 cup shredded coconut,
   optional

Preheat oven to 350 degrees.

In a large bowl, combine cake mix, egg, and butter. Mix in flour. Spread dough thinly to cover a lightly greased jelly roll pan or baking sheet. Bake 10–14 minutes or until lightly golden brown around the edges. Allow to cool completely.

In a medium bowl, mix together powdered sugar, cream cheese, and whipped topping. Spread over cookie layer. Top with sliced fruits. Sprinkle coconut over top, if desired. Store in refrigerator.

Main Course Salads

Country Cobb Salad

Makes 4–6 servings

1 (10-ounce) bag mixed
    salad greens
3 chicken breasts,
    cooked and sliced
1 large tomato, cubed
1/2 cup sliced black
    olives
1 avocado, peeled and
    cubed
4 hard-boiled eggs,
    sliced
12 slices bacon, cooked
    and crumbled
1 cup crumbled blue
    cheese

In a large bowl, layer ingredients as listed. Serve with a dressing of choice on the side. For individual salads, equally divide mixed greens onto plates, then layer with remaining ingredients.

Hearty Grilled Steak Salad

Makes 4–6 *servings*

Marinade

²/₃ cup balsamic
   vinaigrette
1 tablespoon minced
   garlic
1½ teaspoons Italian
   seasoning
¹/₈ teaspoon pepper

1½–2 pounds beef flank
   steak

1 (10-ounce) bag
   romaine salad
1 cup cherry tomatoes,
   halved
1 cup cucumber slices,
   halved
¹/₂ small red onion,
   thinly sliced
1 (2.25-ounce) can
   sliced black olives,
   drained
1 (4-ounce) container
   crumbled feta or blue
   cheese
³/₄ cup balsamic
   vinaigrette

In a 1-gallon ziplock bag, combine marinade ingredients. Add steak to marinade. Zip close, shake to coat steak, and marinate in refrigerator for 6 hours or overnight.

Heat grill. Remove steak from bag and place it on hot grill. Grill for 18–22 minutes turning occasionally until steak reaches desired doneness. On a cutting board, thinly slice steak.

In a large bowl, layer romaine, tomatoes, cucumber, onion, and olives. Place steak slices on top salad. Sprinkle cheese over top. Serve with the balsamic vinaigrette on the side for drizzling over individual servings.

Spicy Taco Salad

Makes 4 servings

1 pound ground beef,
    browned and drained
1 envelope taco
    seasoning
1½ cups chunky salsa
½ teaspoon garlic
    powder
Salt and pepper, to taste
Tortilla chips
2 cups grated cheddar
    cheese
½–1 head iceberg
    lettuce, shredded
2 tomatoes, diced
Sour cream, optional
Guacamole, optional

In a large frying pan, combine cooked beef, taco seasoning, salsa, garlic powder, salt, and pepper until completely heated through.

For individual servings, scoop meat mixture over a bed of tortilla chips on a plate. Layer remaining ingredients over top in order listed above.

VARIATION: Black olives and black beans can also be used in this recipe.

Hawaiian Haystack Salad

3/4 cup mayonnaise
3 tablespoons apple
    cider vinegar
2 tablespoons olive oil
2½ cups cubed cooked
    chicken
2 cups cooked rice
1/2 cup craisins or
    raisins
1 cup chopped celery
1 (11-ounce) can
    mandarin oranges,
    drained
1 (8-ounce) can pine-
    apple tidbits, drained
4–5 green onions,
    chopped
Salted peanuts
Chow mein noodles

In a large bowl, whisk together the mayonnaise, vinegar, and olive oil. Fold in chicken, rice, craisins, celery, oranges, pineapple, and green onions until ingredients are coated. Cover and refrigerate for at least 3 hours or overnight. Garnish individual servings with peanuts and chow mein noodles.

Chinese Chicken Salad

Dressing

1/3 cup water
1/3 cup rice vinegar
1/3 cup olive oil
1 cup sugar
1 packet oriental ramen
  noodle seasoning

Salad

1 head cabbage, thinly
  sliced or shredded
2 stalks celery, sliced
3 packages oriental
  ramen noodles,
  broken up
2 cups cubed cooked
  chicken*
1/2 cup slivered almonds
1/2 cup sunflower seeds

Mix all dressing ingredients in a small bowl and set aside. Combine salad ingredients in a large bowl. Pour dressing over salad and toss until completely covered. Refrigerator 1–2 hours before serving.

*Canned chicken may be used.

Sweet Pork Salad

Makes 4–6 *servings*

1½ pounds boneless
country-style pork
ribs
½ cup sweet barbecue
sauce
½ cup brown sugar
4–6 medium flour
tortillas
Grated cheddar cheese
1 (15-ounce) can black
or pinto beans,
rinsed and drained
1 head romaine lettuce,
torn into bite-size
pieces
Cubed avocado, optional

Creamy Tomatillo Dressing

1 cup buttermilk
½ cup mayonnaise
1 envelope ranch
dressing mix
3–4 fresh tomatillos,
or 1 can whole
tomatillos
1 jalapeño, seeded
1 lime, juiced

Place the pork ribs, barbecue
sauce, and brown sugar in a slow
cooker for 4 hours on high heat, or
8 hours on low heat. When done,
shred with two forks and keep on
low or warm heat. Lay tortillas on
individual serving plates and sprinkle with the cheese and beans. Top
with the lettuce, followed by the
pork and avocado, if using.

To make the dressing, blend all
ingredients in a blender until
smooth. Drizzle the dressing over
the salad and serve.

Crispy Chicken Salad

Makes 4–6 servings

1 (28-ounce) bag frozen
crispy chicken strips
1 (10-ounce) bag
romaine lettuce
$^1/_2$ red onion, thinly
sliced
6–8 hard-boiled eggs,
sliced
12 slices bacon, cooked
and crumbled
2 cups grated sharp
cheddar cheese
Ranch or honey mustard
dressing

Bake chicken according to package directions. Equally divide lettuce onto plates. Layer onion, eggs, bacon, and cheese over top. Evenly divide cooked chicken strips and lay over top. Serve with ranch or honey mustard dressing, or both, on the side.

Ham and Rice Salad

Makes 4–6 *servings*

1½ tablespoons
    prepared mustard
2 tablespoons water
1½ tablespoons sugar
1½ tablespoons vinegar
¼ cup olive oil
1⅓ cups cooked rice
½ cup chopped red bell
    pepper
1 cup cubed cooked ham
½ cup frozen peas,
    thawed

In a medium bowl, whisk together mustard, water, sugar, vinegar, and olive oil until smooth. Fold in cooled rice, bell pepper, and ham. Sprinkle peas over top. Chill until ready to serve. Serve alone or over lettuce.

Chicken Fajita Salad

Makes 4–6 *servings*

1 pound boneless,
  skinless chicken
  breasts, cubed
1 envelope fajita
  seasoning
1 (10-ounce) bag
  romaine lettuce
1 red bell pepper, diced
1 green bell pepper,
  diced
½–1 red onion, thinly
  sliced
1–2 limes, quartered
1 cup grated cheddar or
  pepper jack cheese
Tortilla chips, crushed
Ranch dressing
Salsa

Place chicken in a large ziplock bag. Marinate in fajita seasoning according to package directions.

In a large frying pan, sauté chicken until done. Equally divide lettuce on individual plates, and then evenly sprinkle bell peppers and onion over lettuce. Layer cooked chicken over top. Squeeze lime juice over each salad. Sprinkle cheese and tortilla chips over top. Serve with ranch dressing and salsa on the side.

VARIATION: Layer 1 (15-ounce) can of rinsed and drained black beans over lettuce before chicken is added.

Buffalo Chicken Salad

Makes 4–6 *servings*

1 (28-ounce) bag crispy
    chicken strips
$^1/_3$–$^1/_2$ cup buffalo sauce
1 head romaine lettuce,
    torn into bite-size
    pieces
1 cup Gorgonzola
    crumbles
1 cup sliced celery
Blue cheese or ranch
    dressing

Bake the chicken strips according to package directions; while still warm, cut into bite-size pieces and then toss with the buffalo sauce. On a large platter or on individual plates, layer the lettuce, chicken, cheese, and celery. Serve with dressing on the side.

Chef Salad

2 (10–12-ounce) bags
   mixed salad greens
   or romaine lettuce
2 cups $1/2$-inch strips of
   sliced deli turkey
2 cups $1/2$-inch strips of
   sliced deli ham
$1\frac{1}{2}$ cups grated sharp
   cheddar cheese
$1\frac{1}{2}$ cups grated Monterey
   Jack cheese
2 cups grated carrots
$1\frac{1}{2}$ cups sliced celery
4–6 hard-boiled eggs,
   sliced

For individual salads, equally divide lettuce onto plates, then layer ingredients in the order listed. Serve with dressing of choice.

Grilled Steak and Cherry Salad

Makes 4–6 *servings*

1 large steak, cut of
choice
Balsamic vinegar
Olive oil
Salt and pepper, to taste
$^1/_2$–1 onion, sliced into
thin rings
1 head romaine lettuce,
torn or chopped
20–25 cherries, halved
and pitted
1 cup Gorgonzola cheese
crumbles
Girard's Champagne
Vinaigrette

Brush steak with the vinegar and oil and then sprinkle with salt and pepper; let come to room temperature. Grill to desired doneness in a grill pan or on a barbecue grill; slice into thin strips and set aside.

In a grill pan or on a barbecue grill, grill the onion until browned, about 5 minutes. Divide the lettuce onto 2 plates and then top with equal amounts of steak, onion, cherries, and cheese. Serve with dressing on the side.

Barbecue Chicken Salad

Makes 4–6 *servings*

2 cups French-fried
    onions
1 (10-ounce) bag
    romaine lettuce
1 (15-ounce) can black
    beans, rinsed and
    drained
2 cups grated sharp
    cheddar cheese
1 avocado, diced
1 pound boneless, skin-
    less chicken breasts,
    cooked and cubed
1 cup barbecue sauce
Ranch dressing

To make onions crispy, micro-wave 30 seconds, then set aside. Equally divide lettuce onto individual plates, then layer beans, cheese, avocado. Toss chicken with barbecue sauce and lay over top. Sprinkle onions over all. Serve with ranch dressing on the side.

Marinated Beef Salad

Makes 4–6 *servings*

3/4 pound cooked roast
  beef, sliced
2 tablespoons soy sauce
1 tablespoon sesame
  seeds
1 tablespoon lemon juice
1 clove garlic, crushed
1 small head iceberg or
  leaf lettuce
2 medium tomatoes,
  chopped
2 green onions, sliced
2 cups sliced
  mushrooms
1 (14-ounce) package
  frozen pea pods,
  thawed

Dressing

1/2 cup vegetable oil
1/4 cup apple cider or red
  wine vinegar
1 teaspoon salt
1–2 cloves garlic,
  crushed
Pepper

Marinate beef in soy sauce, sesame
seeds, lemon juice, and garlic for
4 hours in refrigerator.

In a large bowl, toss together every-
thing except dressing ingredients.
Combine dressing ingredients in a
small bowl and pour over salad just
before serving; toss to coat.

Southwest Chicken Caesar Salad

Makes 4 servings

2 chicken breasts, cut into cubes or small strips

4 tablespoons salsa, divided

Dash of Tabasco sauce, optional

1 (10-ounce) bag Dole Caesar Salad kit

1/2 cup pepper jack cheese cubes

1/2 cup diced tomatoes

Tortilla chips or strips, crushed

Marinate the chicken in 3 tablespoons salsa for at least 30 minutes before cooking. Sauté in some olive oil until done; set aside.

Combine the salad kit's Caesar dressing with 1 tablespoon salsa and Tabasco, if desired.

Toss all of the salad ingredients together in a large bowl, leaving out the croutons and cheese packet from the salad kit.

VARIATION: Try adding 1/2 cup black beans or 1/2 cup corn to the salad before tossing.

Jo's Chicken Wonton Salad

Makes 4–6 *servings*

3–4 boneless, skinless chicken breasts, cooked and cubed

1 head iceberg lettuce, chopped

2 cups chopped celery

5 tablespoons toasted sesame seeds

1/4 cup toasted sliced almonds

1 bunch cilantro, chopped

12–14 wonton wrappers, fried in oil and broken up

Dressing

6 tablespoons rice vinegar

2 tablespoons lemon juice

1 teaspoon white pepper

1 1/2 teaspoons dry mustard

1/2 cup oil

1 tablespoon sesame oil

4 tablespoons sugar

1 1/2 teaspoons salt

Toss together all salad ingredients except wontons in a large bowl. Combine all dressing ingredients in a small bowl and then toss onto salad (but don't saturate) just before serving. Add wontons.

Barbecue Chicken and Smoked Gouda Salad

Makes 8–10 *servings*

1 pound grilled chicken
  breasts, cubed
1/2 cup barbecue sauce,
  plus more
1 head leafy green or
  romaine lettuce, torn
  into pieces
4–8 ounces smoked
  Gouda cheese, cut
  into small cubes
1–2 avocados, diced*
1/2 red onion, thinly
  sliced
1/2 cup real bacon bits
Ranch dressing

Toss the cooked chicken in barbecue sauce. Layer the lettuce, chicken, cheese, avocado, onion, and bacon on individual serving plates. Serve with ranch dressing and more barbecue sauce on the side.

*Toss in a little lemon juice to prevent browning.

VARIATION: Add diced tomato or red bell pepper.

Enchilada Salad

Makes 4–6 *servings*

Dressing

1 envelope ranch
    dressing mix
$^1/_2$ cup salsa
$^1/_2$–$^3/_4$ teaspoon Tabasco
    sauce, or to taste

Salad

1 pound boneless, skin-
    less chicken breasts,
    cooked and cubed
$^1/_2$–1 cup enchilada
    sauce
1 head leafy green
    lettuce, torn into
    bite-size pieces
$^1/_2$–1 red onion, thinly
    sliced
1–2 cups grated cheddar
    cheese
1–2 cups crushed Fritos
    corn chips

Make ranch dressing according to package directions. Once dressing is set, combine with salsa and Tabasco sauce and chill until ready to serve.

Toss together the chicken and enchilada sauce.

Layer the lettuce, onion, and chicken on individual plates. Sprinkle cheese and corn chips over top. Serve with spicy ranch dressing on the side.

Turkey Cranberry Salad

1 (10-ounce) bag spring mix lettuce
1–2 cups cubed cooked turkey breast
1 cup grated mozzarella
$^1/_2$–$^3/_4$ cup dried cranberries
$^1/_2$ cup chopped red onion
$^1/_2$ cup sunflower seeds
Poppy seed dressing

In a large bowl, toss all ingredients together except the dressing. Just before serving, toss with desired amount of dressing.

Mango Chicken Salad

Makes 4 servings

1 (10-ounce) bag romaine and iceberg mix salad
2 chicken breasts, grilled and sliced
1 cup dried cranberries
1 mango, peeled and cubed
$^1/_2$ cup slivered almonds
Poppy seed dressing

Place salad on individual plates or bowls, then layer chicken, cranberries, mango, and almonds over top. Serve with poppy seed dressing on the side.

Avocado Chicken Caesar Salad

Makes 4–6 *servings*

1 large avocado
6 cups torn romaine lettuce
1 medium tomato, cut into wedges
2 chicken breasts, grilled and sliced
2–4 tablespoons grated Parmesan cheese
Caesar dressing

Peel avocado, remove pit, and then thinly slice. In a large bowl, gently toss all ingredients except dressing. Serve with dressing on the side or divide all ingredients except dressing and place onto 4–6 salad plates. Place dressing in a small decorative bowl with a small ladle for serving.

VARIATION: Grilled shrimp can be used instead of chicken.

Thai Chicken Salad

Makes 4–6 servings

1 pound chicken, cooked
   and cubed*
1 (14-ounce) bag
   coleslaw salad mix
1 cup sugar snap peas,
   cut into 1-inch
   pieces
1 cup peeled, sliced, and
   quartered cucumber
1 bunch cilantro,
   chopped, divided
2 green onions, sliced
1/2 cup dry-roasted
   peanuts, chopped
1/3 cup lime juice
1 tablespoon rice vinegar
1/3 cup olive oil
1 teaspoon Tabasco sauce

Dressing

2 1/2 tablespoons creamy
   peanut butter
1 1/2 tablespoons rice
   vinegar
1 tablespoon vegetable
   oil
1 tablespoon honey

1 tablespoon water
2 teaspoons soy sauce
2 teaspoons sugar
Salt and ground red
   pepper, to taste
Pinch of red pepper
   flakes

In a large bowl, combine the chicken, coleslaw, peas, cucumber, half the cilantro, green onions, and peanuts; set aside.

In a blender, puree together the remaining cilantro, lime juice, vinegar, oil, and Tabasco. Pour mixture over salad in bowl and toss to coat; set aside.

In a small bowl, combine all of the dressing ingredients and stir until smooth. Pour dressing over salad and stir to combine. Serve.

*Cook chicken in olive oil with salt and pepper and the juice of 1 lime drizzled over top for extra flavor.

Fruit and Nut Chicken Salad

Makes 4–6 *servings*

1 (10-ounce) bag mixed
  salad greens
1 (12.5-ounce) can
  chicken breast meat,
  drained
1 medium apple, cored
  and sliced
1 cup halved seedless
  grapes
1/2 cup chopped walnuts
  or slivered almonds
Honey mustard or ranch
  dressing

Divide salad greens between 4–6 plates. Arrange chicken, apple, grapes, and walnuts over top of each salad. Serve with dressing of choice.

Tortellini Salad

Makes 4–6 servings

Dressing
3/4 cup sugar
3/4 cup mayonnaise
1 tablespoon cider
   vinegar

Salad
2–3 cups bite-size
   broccoli florets
3/4 cup diced roasted red
   peppers
1 pound chicken, cooked
   and cubed
1 (13-ounce) package
   three-cheese
   tortellini, cooked
   and cooled
6–8 slices bacon, cooked
   and crumbled
1/2 cup sunflower seeds
3/4–1 cup crumbled feta
   cheese

In a small bowl, combine sugar, mayonnaise, and cider vinegar until smooth and set aside.

In a large bowl, combine broccoli, red peppers, chicken, cooked tortellini, bacon, sunflower seeds, and cheese. Pour dressing over top and gently stir to coat. Chill 1–2 hours before serving.

Grilled Chicken Chili Salad

Makes 4 servings

4 chicken breast halves, rubbed with olive oil
Chili powder, to taste
Salt and pepper, to taste
Montreal Chicken Seasoning, optional
4 thick slices onion (left as the whole "round" in one piece), rubbed with olive oil
1 small head romaine or leafy green lettuce, torn into bite-size pieces
1 cup frozen corn, thawed
1 (15-ounce) can vegetarian chili, heated
Sour cream
Salsa
Grated cheddar cheese
Texas Toast Chili Lime Tortilla Strips or Tostitos Chips with Lime

Sprinkle the chicken with the chili powder, salt, pepper, and chicken seasoning on both sides. Grill chicken and onion on the barbecue grill until done. Slice the chicken into thin pieces and cut the onion slices into quarters so you have bite-size strips.

Divide lettuce onto 4 individual plates and sprinkle with corn, followed by the grilled onion. Lay the sliced chicken down the center and then top with one-fourth of the chili. Add sour cream and salsa over the chili and then top with the cheese and tortilla strips or crushed chips.

Chopped Chicken and Dried Cherry Salad

Makes 4 servings

4–6 chicken tenders, seasoned with Montreal Chicken Seasoning

1 head romaine lettuce, chopped

1 stalk celery, chopped

1/2 cucumber, peeled and chopped

1/3 red onion, chopped

4–6 slices bacon, cooked and chopped

4 ounces extra sharp white cheddar cheese, cut into small pieces or cubes

3/4 cup dried cherries, roughly chopped

3/4 cup cashews, roughly chopped

Brianna's Blush Wine Vinaigrette or balsamic vinaigrette

On a barbecue grill or in a grill pan, grill the seasoned chicken until done; let cool slightly and then chop or slice.

In a large bowl or on individual serving plates, pile on the lettuce, celery, cucumber, and onion. Sprinkle some of the chicken down the center of the salad and then top with the bacon, cheese, cherries, and cashews. Top with the vinaigrette.

Chicken and Wild Rice Salad

Makes 6–8 *servings*

1 cup uncooked wild rice, cooked according to directions

3–4 tablespoons lemon juice (or more if needed)

2 cups cubed rotisserie chicken

1 red bell pepper, diced

1½ cups sugar snap peas, cut into pieces

1 cup chopped pecan halves

2 avocados, cut into chunks

Dressing

2 cloves garlic, minced

1 tablespoon Dijon mustard

½ teaspoon salt

¼ teaspoon pepper

¼ cup sugar

¼ cup red wine or apple cider vinegar

⅓ cup vegetable or olive oil

Rinse the cooked rice and then toss with the lemon juice in a large bowl; let cool completely. Stir in the chicken, bell pepper, peas, and nuts.

Combine the dressing ingredients in a small bowl and then toss in the salad mixture along with the avocado.

Dessert
Salads

Fluffy Lime Salad

Makes 6 servings

1 large box lime gelatin
1 cup boiling water
1 (5-ounce) can
    evaporated milk,
    very cold*
2 cups crushed graham
    crackers, divided

Dissolve lime gelatin in boiling water in a medium bowl then refrigerate 20–25 minutes, or until it starts to set. Pour milk into a large chilled bowl and whip with chilled beaters until mixture forms stiff peaks, about 5 minutes. Gently stir in gelatin mixture until well blended.

Sprinkle half the graham crackers into bottom of an 8 x 8-inch pan then carefully spoon lime fluff over top and spread evenly, being careful not to pull up graham cracker crumbs. Sprinkle remaining graham cracker crumbs over top and refrigerate 1–2 hours before serving.

*Chill by placing can in freezer 20–30 minutes.

Fudgy Cookies and Cream Salad

Makes 6–8 servings

2 cups whipping
 cream, whipped
 and sweetened
1 large box chocolate
 fudge instant pud-
 ding, made according
 to directions
15–20 Oreo cookies,
 crushed

In a large bowl, gently fold the whipped cream into the prepared pudding. Fold in the cookie crumbles. Refrigerate at least 2 hours before serving. Garnish with a large dollop of whipped cream and whole Oreos, if desired.

Pistachio Salad

Makes 6–8 servings

1 small box instant
 pistachio pudding
1 (8-ounce) can crushed
 pineapple, with juice
1 (8-ounce) container
 whipped topping,
 thawed
2–3 cups miniature
 marshmallows
1 cup cottage cheese
Chopped pistachios

Combine pudding mix and pineapple with juice together in a large bowl. Stir in whipped topping, marshmallows, and cottage cheese. Garnish with pistachios. Refrigerate 1–2 hours before serving.

Dreamy Gelatin Salad

Makes **8–10** *servings*

1 large box gelatin,
    any flavor
2 cups boiling water
1 cup cold water
1 (8-ounce) package
    cream cheese,
    softened
1 cup vanilla ice cream,
    softened
1 (8-ounce) container
    frozen whipped
    topping, thawed
    and divided
Crushed graham
    crackers, optional

Mix gelatin and boiling water together in a large bowl until dissolved. Add cold water, cream cheese, ice cream, and half the whipped topping. Mix with a hand mixer until creamy and smooth. Pour mixture into a 9 x 13-inch pan and refrigerate 2–3 hours. Top with remaining whipped topping. Sprinkle crushed graham crackers over top as a garnish, if desired.

Graham Family's Sunshine Salad

Makes **10–12** *servings*

1 large box cook-and-serve lemon pudding
1 small box orange gelatin
2 cups hot water

Topping

1 small box instant lemon pudding
1 cup milk
1 (8-ounce) container frozen whipped topping, thawed
1 (11-ounce) can mandarin oranges, drained

In a large saucepan, cook pudding according to package directions. Stir in dry gelatin and hot water. Combine well and pour into a 9 x 13-inch glass pan. Chill for 4–5 hours or overnight.

In a large bowl, whisk together the dry pudding mix and milk. Fold whipped topping into pudding until blended. Spread whipped topping mixture over salad. Lay orange segments evenly over top. Chill until ready to serve.

Banana Cream Salad

Makes 10–12 servings

2 small boxes banana
   cream pudding
3½ cups milk
30 vanilla wafers,
   divided
2 bananas, sliced
1 (8-ounce) container
   frozen whipped
   topping, thawed

Prepare pudding with milk by following the pie preparation directions on package. Pour half the pudding into a 9 x 13-inch pan. Break 20 wafers into bite-size pieces evenly over pudding. Pour remaining pudding over top. Chill until set. When ready to serve slice bananas and layer over pudding. Spread whipped topping over bananas, then break remaining wafers over top.

Citrus Cream Salad

Makes 8–10 servings

1 large box cook-and-
   serve lemon pudding
1 large box orange
   gelatin
1 (8-ounce) container
   frozen whipped
   topping, thawed

Make pudding according to package directions in a large bowl and set aside, keeping warm.

In a medium bowl, make gelatin according to package directions. While gelatin is still warm, pour into warm pudding and mix well. Pour into a 9 x 13-inch pan and chill 3–4 hours, or until set. Spread a thick layer of whipped topping over top.

Lemon-Lime Cream Salad

Makes 10–12 servings

1 large box cook-and-
serve lemon pudding
1 large box lime gelatin
1 (8-ounce) container
frozen whipped
topping, thawed

In a large saucepan, make pudding following package directions. Remove pudding from heat.

In a small bowl, make gelatin following package directions. Stir warm gelatin mixture into pan of warm pudding. Pour mixture into a 9 x 13-inch glass pan with tall sides. Refrigerate 4–5 hours or overnight. Just before serving, spread whipped topping over top.

Cherry-Pineapple Salad

Makes 10–12 servings

1 (21-ounce) can cherry
pie filling
1 (20-ounce) can crushed
pineapple, drained
1 (14-ounce) can sweet-
ened condensed milk
1½ cups miniature
marshmallows
1 (8-ounce) container
frozen whipped
topping, thawed

In a large bowl, combine the pie filling, pineapple, condensed milk, and marshmallows. Gently fold in whipped topping. Garnish with fresh cherries or chopped pecans, if desired. Chill until ready to serve.

Best Ever Frog-Eye Salad

Makes 10–12 servings

1½ cups ancini di pepe pasta

1 cup sugar

½ teaspoon salt

2 tablespoons flour

3 egg yolks

1½ cups pineapple juice (drained from can)*

1–2 (20-ounce) cans pineapple tidbits, drained with juice reserved

2 (11-ounce) cans mandarin oranges, drained

1 (16-ounce) bag miniature marshmallows

1 (12-ounce) container frozen whipped topping, thawed

Boil pasta according to package directions, then drain, rinse, and cool.

Combine sugar, salt, flour, egg yolks, and pineapple juice in a small saucepan and cook over medium heat until slightly thickened.

In a large bowl, combine pasta and sauce and stir; chill 6 hours. Add pineapple, mandarin oranges, marshmallows, and whipped topping. Refrigerate 1–2 hours before serving.

*If pineapple juice drained from cans doesn't measure 1½ cups, combine with juice drained from mandarin oranges.

Rocky Road Salad

Makes 6–8 servings

**1 large box instant
chocolate pudding**
**4 ounces frozen whipped
topping, thawed**
**2½ cups miniature
marshmallows**
¾ cup chopped walnuts
**½ cup mini chocolate
chips**

Make pudding according to package directions in a large bowl and chill until set. Fold in whipped topping then stir in remaining ingredients.

Snickers Salad

Makes 6–8 servings

**5 Snickers bars, cut into
bite-size pieces**
**4 Fuji apples, cut into
bite-size pieces**
**1 (8-ounce) container
frozen whipped
topping, thawed**
**Caramel ice cream
topping**

Mix all ingredients together in a large bowl except caramel topping and chill. Lightly drizzle caramel over top just before serving.

Pumpkin Gingersnap Cookie Salad

Makes 10–12 *servings*

35 gingersnap cookies, crushed and divided

1 small box instant butterscotch pudding

1/2 cup cold milk

4 cups vanilla bean ice cream or frozen vanilla yogurt, softened

1 cup canned pumpkin

1/4 teaspoon pumpkin pie spice

Place all but 1/4 cup cookie crumbs over the bottom of a 9 x 13-inch glass pan.

In a medium bowl, beat together the dry pudding and milk until smooth. Beat in ice cream, pumpkin, and pumpkin pie spice until well blended. Pour and spread pudding mixture evenly over crumb layer. Sprinkle remaining crumbs over top. Refrigerate before and after serving.

NOTE: Sugar-free pudding and light or sugar-free ice cream or frozen yogurt can be substituted.

Pineapple Sherbet Salad

Makes 10–12 servings

1 (12-ounce) bag frozen
    raspberries, slightly
    thawed
1/2 gallon pineapple
    sherbet, slightly
    softened
2–3 bananas
Fresh raspberries,
    optional

Mash raspberries into softened sherbet then slice bananas and gently stir in. Serve in parfait glasses. Garnish with a few fresh raspberries, if desired.

Berry Lemon Pudding Salad

Makes 10–12 servings

1 large box cook-and-
    serve lemon pudding
1 small box cranberry
    gelatin
1 small box raspberry
    gelatin
1 (8-ounce) container
    frozen whipped
    topping, thawed
Fresh raspberries

In a large saucepan, make lemon pudding following the pie directions.

In separate small bowls, make gelatins according to package directions. Stir warm gelatin mixtures into warm pudding. Pour into a 9 x 13-inch glass pan. Refrigerate 3 hours or overnight. Just before serving, spread whipped topping over top. Garnish with fresh raspberries.

Layered Strawberry Shortcake Salad

Makes 8–10 servings

1 box Strawberry Danish
   Dessert, prepared
   according to "Fruit
   Sauce" directions
4 cups sliced
   strawberries
1 loaf angel food cake,
   cut into 1-inch cubes
1 (8-ounce) container
   frozen whipped
   topping, thawed

Combine the prepared Danish and strawberries in a medium bowl and refrigerate for 1 hour.

In a large glass bowl or trifle dish, place half the cake cubes. Top with half the strawberry mixture and half the Cool Whip. Repeat layers. Refrigerate at least 1 hour before serving.

Tropical Ambrosia Salad

Makes 6-8 servings

1 (15-ounce) can
  mandarin oranges,
  drained
1 (8-ounce) can crushed
  pineapple, drained
1¼ cups coconut
2 cups miniature
  marshmallows
1 (8-ounce) container
  frozen whipped
  topping, thawed

In a large serving bowl, combine oranges, pineapple, coconut, and marshmallows. Gently stir whipped topping into salad. Chill for at least 1 hour before serving. Garnish with chopped pecans or maraschino cherries, if desired.

NOTE: This recipe can be made the night before serving.

Peachy Parfait Salad

Makes 8-10 servings

1 large box peach
  gelatin
2 cups boiling water
1½ cups cold water
1 (15-ounce) can sliced
  peaches, drained
1½ cups miniature
  marshmallows
1 (8-ounce) container
  frozen whipped
  topping, thawed

In a large bowl, stir gelatin into boiling water until dissolved. Stir in cold water. Refrigerate 2 hours or overnight. Chop gelatin into small pieces and place in a large bowl. Dice peaches into bite-size pieces. Stir peaches, marshmallows, and whipped topping into gelatin. Chill until ready to serve.

Grandma's Strawberry Pretzel Salad

Makes 10–12 servings

2 cups chopped pretzels
2/3 cup butter or margarine, melted
4 tablespoons sugar
1 (8-ounce) package cream cheese, softened
1 cup sugar
1 (8-ounce) container frozen whipped topping, thawed
2 small boxes strawberry gelatin
1½ cups boiling water
2 (10-ounce) cartons frozen strawberries in syrup, thawed

Preheat oven to 400 degrees.

Mix pretzels, butter, and sugar together. Press into bottom of a 9 x 13-inch glass pan. Bake 6 minutes and then cool.

In a large bowl, mix the cream cheese, sugar, and whipped topping. Spread over pretzel crust. In a medium bowl, combine strawberry gelatin and boiling water until gelatin dissolves. Stir in strawberries and spread mixture over cream layer. Chill 3–4 hours until set.

VARIATION: Raspberries and raspberry gelatin may be used instead of strawberries and strawberry gelatin.

Grandma Dirck's Orange Cream Salad

Makes 8–10 servings

1 small box orange gelatin
1 small box cook-and-serve vanilla pudding
1 small box tapioca pudding
3 cups cold water
1 (11-ounce) can mandarin oranges, drained
1 (12-ounce) container frozen whipped topping, thawed

In a medium saucepan, combine the gelatin, puddings, and water. Bring to a boil, stirring constantly, and boil for 2 minutes; remove from heat and cool to room temperature. Stir in oranges. Transfer salad to a large glass bowl. Gently fold in whipped topping, reserving a dollop to garnish top. Refrigerate until ready to serve.

Tropical Cookie Salad

Makes 8–10 servings

2 small boxes instant
    vanilla pudding
2 cups buttermilk
1 (12-ounce) container
    frozen whipped
    topping, thawed
1 (20-ounce) can crushed
    pineapple, drained
2 bananas, sliced
2 (11-ounce) cans
    mandarin oranges,
    drained
1/2 (11.5-ounce) package
    fudge-striped cookies

In a large bowl, combine the pudding and buttermilk. Gently fold whipped topping into pudding mixture. Stir in pineapple, bananas, and oranges. Chill until ready to serve. Just before serving, break cookies into bite-size pieces and sprinkle over salad.

VARIATIONS: In place of fudge-striped cookies, sprinkle crushed chocolate sandwich cookies or Twix candy bars, cut into bite-size pieces, over salad before serving.

Cookies and Cream Pudding Salad

Makes 8–10 servings

2 small boxes instant vanilla pudding
2 cups buttermilk
1 (16-ounce) container frozen whipped topping, thawed
2 (11-ounce) cans mandarin oranges, drained
24 Oreo cookies, chopped

In a large bowl, whisk together the dry pudding mix and buttermilk until smooth. Fold in whipped topping until well blended. Fold in oranges. Cover and chill until ready to serve. Just before serving, stir in chopped cookies.

Pineapple Pretzel Salad

Makes 10–12 servings

2 cups crushed pretzels

2/3 cup butter or
    margarine, melted

1 cup sugar, divided

1 (20-ounce) can crushed
    pineapple, with juice

2 tablespoons
    cornstarch

1 (8-ounce) package
    cream cheese,
    softened

1 (8-ounce) container
    frozen whipped
    topping, thawed

Preheat oven to 400 degrees.

Combine pretzels, butter, and 1/2 cup sugar in a medium bowl. Press into bottom of a 9 x 13-inch glass pan. Bake for 6 minutes; let cool.

In a small saucepan, combine pineapple with juice, remaining sugar, and cornstarch. Bring to a boil, stirring constantly. Allow pineapple mixture to cool. Spread cooled pineapple mixture over pretzel crust. Mix cream cheese and whipped topping together in a medium bowl and spread over pineapple mixture. Chill for 2 hours or overnight. Garnish with chopped nuts, if desired.

Layered Lemon Cranberry Cream Salad

Makes 10–12 servings

- 1 small box instant vanilla pudding
- 1 small box lemon gelatin
- 2 cups water
- 2 tablespoons lemon juice
- 1 small box cranberry or raspberry gelatin
- 1 cup boiling water
- 1 (16-ounce) can jellied cranberry sauce
- $^1/_2$ teaspoon nutmeg
- 1 (8-ounce) container frozen whipped topping, thawed
- Chopped pecans, optional

In a small saucepan, combine the pudding mix, lemon gelatin, and water. Bring to a boil, stirring constantly. Remove from heat and stir in lemon juice. Transfer to a large bowl and chill at least 1 hour, or until partially set.

After placing pudding mixture in refrigerator, dissolve cranberry gelatin in boiling water in a medium bowl. Stir in cranberry sauce until well blended; chill until partially set.

Gently stir nutmeg into whipped topping and then fold into cold pudding mixture. Pour into a glass bowl or a 9 x 13-inch glass pan; chill until firm. Spread cranberry mixture evenly over pudding layer. Chill for at least 5–6 hours before serving. Garnish with chopped pecans, if desired.

Bonus Section: Dressings

Creamy Poppy Seed Dressing

1/2 cup mayonnaise
1/4 cup milk
1/4 cup sugar
2–3 tablespoons red
   wine vinegar
1 tablespoon poppy seeds

With a whisk, combine all ingredients together in a small bowl. Refrigerate 1–2 hours before serving. Store dressing in refrigerator.

Mom's Western Dressing

1 cup ketchup
1 cup vegetable or olive
   oil
3/4 cup vinegar
1 1/4 cups sugar
1/2 teaspoon ground
   mustard
1/2 teaspoon paprika
1 teaspoon salt
1/4 teaspoon garlic
   powder
1/2 teaspoon barbecue
   seasoning

Combine all ingredients in a blender. Refrigerate 1–2 hours before serving. Store dressing in refrigerator.

Honey Mustard Dressing

1 (6-ounce) container
   plain yogurt
1/3 cup light mayonnaise
1/3 cup honey
1/4 cup Dijon mustard
2 tablespoons mustard
4 1/2 teaspoons cider
   vinegar

With a whisk, combine all ingredients together in a small bowl. Refrigerate 1–2 hours before serving. Store dressing in refrigerator.

Creamy Italian Dressing

1/4 teaspoon oregano
1/4 teaspoon garlic
1/4 teaspoon onion
   powder
1 cup low-fat cottage
   cheese
1/3 cup buttermilk
1 teaspoon lemon juice

Combine all ingredients together in a blender. Chill until ready to serve. Store dressing in refrigerator.

Creamy Parmesan Dressing

1/4 cup milk
1 cup light mayonnaise
2 tablespoons vinegar
3 tablespoons grated
  Parmesan cheese

With a whisk, combine all ingredients together in a small bowl. Refrigerate 1–2 hours before serving. Store dressing in refrigerator.

Quick French Dressing

1 (10.75-ounce) can condensed tomato soup
1 cup sugar
1 cup vegetable or olive oil
1 cup vinegar

Combine all ingredients in the blender. Chill until ready to serve. Store dressing in refrigerator.

Lime Vinaigrette

1/4 cup light olive oil
1/4 cup lime juice
2 teaspoons sugar
1/2 teaspoon grated lime peel
1/4 teaspoon salt

With a whisk, combine all ingredients together in a small bowl. Store dressing in refrigerator.

Favorite Herb Vinaigrette

$1/2$ **cup light olive oil**
$1/4$ **cup sugar**
**3 tablespoons cider
    vinegar**
**1 tablespoon minced
    fresh parsley**
$1/2$ **teaspoon salt**
$1/4$ **teaspoon pepper**

With a whisk, combine all ingredients together in a small bowl. Store dressing in refrigerator.

Red Wine Vinaigrette

$1/2$ **cup vegetable oil**
$1/2$ **cup red wine vinegar**
$1/4$–$1/3$ **cup sugar**
**2 teaspoons Dijon
    mustard**
$1/2$ **teaspoon oregano**
$1/4$ **teaspoon pepper**

With a whisk, combine all ingredients together in a small bowl. Store dressing in refrigerator.

Index